MANAGING
A STARTUP
IN THE DIGITAL AGE

Howard A. Tullman

BLOG into**BOOK**

Published in the United States of America
For bulk orders, please contact info@blogintobook.com

Cover design portrait courtesy of Matthew Cherry
Perspiration Principles logo designed by James "Red" Schmitt
Special Thanks to Lakshmi Shenoy and Claudia Saric

To purchase "Tullman on Company Culture," please visit:
BlogIntoBook.com/companyculture/

ISBN: 9781619849778

DEDICATION

Sitting down every week to write something that will be meaningful and ideally of lasting value to others is a lot like setting out to start a new business. Sometimes there's a germ of an idea; sometimes it's an emotional reaction or other driver; or perhaps it's just a problem or situation that needs to be addressed. And occasionally you simply want to see things change and no one else is stepping up to the plate to make that happen.

You can't know how hard, long or costly (in many ways) the journey will be and there are no guarantees that anything good will ever come of your efforts, but you know for certain that nothing will ever happen if you don't get the process started and try. It's a lonely path and every bit of encouragement, assistance and support that you find along the way makes the job a little easier and slightly more likely to succeed.

I hope that these books will be my modest contribution to your success and to the well-worn and tattered bag of hopes and dreams which we call entrepreneurship.

CONTENTS

JOB JUMPERS NEED NOT APPLY

I've said for many years that ultimately technology is not a long-term sustainable competitive advantage because – as the cost of any new technology continues to plummet (which it eventually does in every case) – it becomes a commodity that is readily affordable and available to anyone in the marketplace. So what is it that sets the best businesses apart – regardless of their size – or any momentary advantages which their latest technologies may provide? It's their people – dedicated, passionate, committed and hard-working - that ultimately will make the difference between success and so-what. Finding, attracting, hiring, retaining and fairly compensating the best and brightest folks you can locate is the only way to assure your future.

And that's true in part because it's almost never the technology itself that makes the critical difference anyway – it's the smart application by the members of your team of these technologies to solve important and substantial business problems that will set your company apart from the rest. In many cases, the technologies and the problems have been around for a long time; what was missing in the past was the clear and new vision, the inspirational spark, and the guts and initiative to make a change.

And - while there are certainly cases where the invention of new technologies opens doors and possibilities which we never before even contemplated – as often as not – most of the new, game-changing applications aren't instances of any special rocket science (the technologies are typically already built, stable and even industrial-strength as well as readily scalable); they're simply cases of having talented people who see things differently (than everyone else has in the past) applying what are often very simple and basic technologies in ways that accelerate, improve and enhance traditional processes and solutions in order to save time or money (or both) and increase their customers' productivity.

Easy to explain; hard to execute. And it always starts with people. But it's not simply about super smart people. It's about having the people with the right mindset and attitude. People who want to stick around and do the heavy lifting that it takes to make a difference and build a real business. Things that don't happen in a flash or overnight. The truth is that an ounce of loyalty these days is worth a pound of cleverness because, in the tech space these days, we have a highly mobile workforce with fewer geographic ties than ever before, less practical constraints, commitments and obligations (other than student debt), and a much higher propensity to jump from job to job – often for the cash and the perks – but just as often it would seem for the sheer cumulating of diverse work experiences.

So, especially for new, young companies, the singly most crucial component of the entire HR equation is retention. That's why it's so great to build a business in Chicago where people better understand and appreciate the meaning and value of a long-term commitment as opposed to the Valley where everything seems to be about quick scores and compensation. Frankly, if your employees are always looking for their next job, a new title, and a bump in their comp; they're not taking care of your business in the way they should.

But, here again, too many companies make the mistake of thinking that increasing retention is a product of something that you can actively do "to" people. This is the same fallacious reasoning that leads old time college professors to think that the measure of their success is what and how they teach when, in fact, it's what their students learn that really matters. Today, no one commits to a company anymore – they commit to other talented people whom they want to work with; they commit to solving challenging and substantial problems; and – in the best places – they commit to ideas that are bigger and more important than themselves.

These are fundamentally internal and often emotional (not necessarily rational) considerations – not something that's driven by décor, desserts, drinks or dogma – and not something that the company can manufacture or manipulate. You need to have people in your business who are loyal beyond reason because building a new business is just that tough – everyday tough – in every way. And real results aren't ever the product of rules and regulations and orders- they're the product of commitment and – even more importantly – of perseverance. So if your workers have one foot out the door and their eyes on some other prize, you're not building the foundation that you'll need for the future.

It's a funny thing – when you're first starting your business – when it's just an idea; it's all about story and contagious enthusiasm. But as you start building your business; it's all about the long haul – perseverance, perspiration and execution. To win over time takes character – to bear up when things are going south or sideways – takes grit and heart. And it takes a firm and full commitment – not a drive-by or toe in the water approach – and not just in words or cheap talk – but in an all-in spirit. It's like an eggs and bacon breakfast. The chicken makes a contribution; the pig makes a commitment.

So ultimately, it comes down to this. You can set the stage; you can create the surroundings; and you can certainly say all the right things, but you can't make the ultimate commitment for anyone but yourself. And there are very few tools to help you in this process – there are no spreadsheets or budget line items or litmus tests for these kinds of strengths and choices. Although when you've been at it for a while, it's easier than you would think to figure out who's not a keeper. So what is it that you can do to tip the scales in your favor?

In the end, all you can really do – as Bruce Springsteen would say - is to try to make an honest stand. Tell your people what you're trying to accomplish and why. Tell them what you're willing to sacrifice in order to accomplish that goal and what you expect of them as well. Tell them the truth and the costs of getting there – whatever those costs may be. And hang on dearly to the ones who step forward and sign up.

MAKE ROOM FOR PEOPLE – PART 1

As your company grows, the most important and hardest decisions that you will make will be about the people you hire and those you have to fire. There's a lot of talk these days about technology, but some things never change and the fact of the matter is that the ONE sustainable competitive advantage that any business can have for the long run is talented, committed and passionate people. Everything else erodes over time – especially technology which eventually in every case becomes accessible, cheaper and more broadly applicable by your competitors

Many years ago I made this chart to track the price-novelty curve of technology which shows how the price of new technology diminishes over time and the other marketplace changes that accompany this process. (You'll get some idea of how old this chart is by noting that the software I used couldn't really even replicate a smooth curve.)

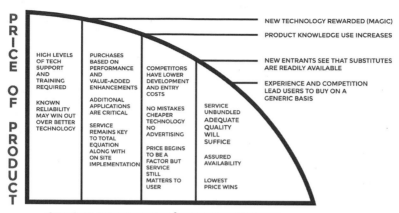

STAGES OF NOVELTY/DIFFERENTATION

As you can see from the chart, while at the outset, new technology is almost indistinguishable from magic, by the time it becomes widely available and accepted, people basically take it for granted and price drives the discussion. As you can imagine, discussions about the lowest available price are never what we would call "happy talk".

But, good people, well-educated and motivated, just get better, stronger and more valuable all the time – especially if you watch their backs and stay out of their way. The real trick is to find 'em, hire 'em and keep 'em. Equally important is to move quickly to fire the people who aren't making it. Simple rule: Hire slow; fire fast.

(I'll deal with keeping your top performers and firing people who aren't in the next couple of posts, but suffice it to say that virtually NO ONE was ever fired too soon. Once you know that things aren't working out, you almost can't move too quickly to fix the situation. Every day you wait is one day too many and much too late.)

Let me start with a piece of bad news that comes from my friend Jay Goltz who says that CEOs are among the worst possible people to do their company's hiring. Why? Because, by and large, they're (a) short on time and often distracted; (b) great talkers and bad listeners because they're always selling themselves and their businesses rather than asking and learning about the interviewee; and (c) too good-natured and trusting about people and not skeptical enough to ask the hard questions. So you may not be the best person in your organization to do this job even though there are few that are more important.

So consider yourself warned. Now, what can you do to at least give yourself a fighting chance of doing a good job? Here are a few ideas and rules that have helped me over the years:

(1) <u>People lie about their resumes all the time.</u>

I'm not saying this to get you down on mankind in general or anything like that. I'm just suggesting that it's perfectly reasonable to ask detailed questions about a resume and to take everything on it with a grain of salt or a tablespoon. I looked younger than my age for years (not sure when things caught up) and I once flew to France for a huge meeting with some folks over there involving millions of dollars. I got there – walked into the room – and was treated so shabbily by these folks (even taking into account that they were French assholes) that I was dumbfounded. I had lunch and went right back to the airport and returned home. I later learned that they saw me and having read my pretty extensive resume decided that I wasn't old enough to have done half the stuff written there and so I must have been lying to them. I wasn't, but it was a real lesson in managing information and expectations that I've never forgotten.

(2) <u>Credentials are not the same as accomplishments.</u>

Degrees are nice to have, but it's your deeds and the things you've actually gotten done that matter in the final analysis. And, there are plenty of "smart" people out there who aren't people smart. If you can't get along with the "natives" as part of an effective and collaborative team, your native intelligence doesn't mean squat.

(3) The best person you interview may not be the best person for the job in question.

Too many CEOs think that they should hire any great person who comes along and figure out a good job for them later. As important as it is to have super-talented people, trying to "warehouse" them (even when you're growing like crazy) is a losing strategy. Get a clear job description, understand the criteria for a successful candidate, and focus on filling that job.

(4) There are no easy jobs today. Every candidate should have the basic required skills as a starting point.

But the right prospects are the ones who have the ability to get the job done. Ability in any area is the successful combination of toughness (mental and physical), resourcefulness (flexibility and adaptability) and powerful concentration (focus and direction).

(5) Gray hair is a sign of age, not necessarily wisdom or relevant experience.

Young and (first-time) CEOs tend to get a point in the early growth of their businesses where they believe that they need to add some "grown-ups" to the management mix. There are usually a number of pretty standard excuses, explanations and reasons offered for these kinds of feelings, but ultimately the real driver is fear: (a) fear of being alone and responsible; (b) fear of being in way over your head; and (c) fear of fucking things up. I can't make the fears go away, but I can tell you that 90 times out of 100 these types of lateral hires fail miserably and you will be the most miserable of all concerned because you did it to yourself and your company. There's not a simple or single explanation for the overwhelming failure rate, but generally the 4 main misses are: (1) a quickly-emergent lack of energy (stamina) and enthusiasm; (2) a totally absent connection to and comfort with the rest of the employees; (3) an early tendency to criticize the way you run the business; and (4) a focus and excessive interest in and emphasis on financial and compensation issues.

MAKE ROOM FOR PEOPLE - PART 2

Once you've hired some terrific people, the next job is to hang on to them. Interestingly enough, that's getting harder, not easier, to do even in these tough economic times because (a) no one assumes any longer that they'll spend most of their career at the same place and (b) people these days don't commit to companies, they commit to other people and other people change and move on all the time. So how can you keep the stars (and the rest of the troops) happy, healthy and motivated?

First, nothing is more important than making room for people. All kinds of people – because talent comes in lots of different sizes, shapes and packages. We want the talent, but we aren't always willing to understand that it's a package deal. Some people like to work all night; some don't especially care to bath; some are insufferable and brilliant at the same time. You need to make room for these people and run interference for them if you want to build a great company. Too often, entrepreneurs try to find and hire people that look, act and talk like them and this never works beyond the first few employees. You need all kinds of people – even people just looking for a job – not a career and not looking to join your sacred crusade – just as long as they're willing to do their job and do it as well as they can. And honestly, your employees also don't have to love each other or go bowling every Thursday night. They just all need to show up and each do their jobs. Everything else is Kumbaya and gravy.

Second, you've got to talk straight to everyone, tell the truth, and do a couple of administrative things right away: (1) define and nail down each new person's job and the reporting hierarchy; (2) explain your expectations – tell people what you're trying to accomplish and what you're willing to sacrifice to accomplish it and make sure that they're signed up for the same trip; and (3) establish the criteria to measure and evaluate success and confirm in writing that they are understood by everyone.

It's funny, but over the years, you learn that that the people from whom you really learned the real things of value (good or bad) were not the warm and fuzzy folks. They were sharp, hard-edged, driven people with a clear sense of purpose who were always asking more of you. And the real reason that those times were so instructive was that, in the midst of all of the blood, sweat and tears, and occasional screaming, you never doubted for a moment that they believed in you and believed that you were up to the task and could do whatever it took to get it done AND you knew that they would be there working and standing right beside you when you did.

It's great to shoot for the sky and have high expectations and to ask your people to work insane hours and move mountains as long as you never ask them to do anything that you wouldn't do yourself and as long as you're working side-by-side just as hard as they are. This whole area is a slippery slope. Keep in mind that getting the most work out of people isn't necessarily getting their best work. Ultimately, it's a quality, not simply a quantity game. Lots of people learn how to keep busy – the trick is to get things done and done right. Not all movement is progress.

Third, forget all this bullshit that every idea is a good one. Plenty of ideas just suck. Pretending that every idea is possible or worthy of consideration and discussion and trying to be politically correct and always constructive in your criticism is a formula for failure. It's nice to be liked; it's more important to be respected. And sympathy is a lot like junk food – it doesn't help anybody to lie to people or give them false encouragement or hope. Hurt feelings, bruised egos, skinned knees are all part of the growth process and critical to it.

Finally, your people are very important, but don't lose sight of the main chance. The name of the game is to create great products and services and to build a company that will last – it's really not about making people feel good about themselves and loved. Leave that to the clergy. Seeking consensus is about finding the middle ground, settling, and making people feel good about themselves and each other – it's a completely different objective than building your business and it has no place in the rough and tumble world of getting a new company off the ground. You can have higher aspirations, broader goals, and apple pie mission statements once you can pay the bills and afford those luxuries.

In much the same way, teamwork is certainly a wonderful thing, but in a start-up, it's mainly a means to getting the help you need to see your vision through to completion. Political correctness, consensus building and hyper-collaborative teamwork will only take you so far. You can't serve too many masters or chase too many rabbits at the same time or you'll end up with none. You're not a social welfare agency; you're not a church or a charity; and you're not your employees' shrink or family – you're a small, young business trying to grow into something important and that alone is a full-time job and then some.

The truth is that most of the world's great products and businesses – as well as most of the great inventions throughout history – were ultimately the result and expression of a single, uncompromising vision - albeit managed, massaged, and manipulated through a sea of change, confusion and compromise. That's your main job – define, defend and drive the vision. The reason that it's so important to always keep the vision front and center and so inextricably tied to your people is that great ideas can bring people, but ultimately it's something bigger – ideals – that keeps them together. We all want to be working for something that's bigger than ourselves.

In building your business, you have a small window and often a single chance, a passing moment and a fleeting opportunity to make something special and spectacular and to make a difference – if you have the courage of your convictions, the confidence in your abilities, and if you're willing to make and stick to the hard choices that will inevitably arise. The people choices are always the hardest.

MAKE ROOM FOR PEOPLE – PART 3

There's no more challenging job in a young company than being the person who has to let people go. Everyone else gets to talk about what a tight-knit, stick together group the company is (just like a "family" of friends) and all that other touchy-feely stuff, but you're the one who has to deliver the bad news over and over again. And it's true whether you're the CEO or the head of sales or the HR manager – it doesn't really matter – it's a tough job for anyone. If you were unpopular in high school, you're already one step ahead of the game. It's not easy or always popular to be the boss, but then good leadership isn't a popularity contest. It's a given that you can't please any of the people all the time.

The truth is that your company's only as good as your worst employee and the best-run businesses are always looking to either retrain and upgrade or replace the lowest performing employees. Sometimes it's a breeze. We try to immediately fire any employee who doesn't try or doesn't care. These are cardinal sins in a start-up and there's no question that these people need to go – they're always the easiest decisions. And then the job gets harder and harder.

The next tier of troublesome employees is those who try hard, but just cannot do the job. You can be totally sincere and have the best of intentions, but still be incapable (or no longer capable) of doing the job that needs to get done. There are good people who are perfectly able to do a job poorly for a very long time before anyone has the time, interest, or guts to ask the hard questions about results rather than effort. These people need to go too, but you need to be as fair and firm with them as you can. And do them a real favor – tell them the truth.

Then there are the employees who are basically hard-working and dedicated, but who (for better or worse) can't fit into or model the corporate culture and behaviors. Every business that I've been involved with has ultimately been about hard work mixed in with a healthy dose of paranoia. We had lots of ways to reflect this ethic and plenty of signs all over the place. "Hard work conquers everything." "Effort can trump ability." "We may not outsmart them, but we'll outwork them every time." "Obstacles are those frightful little things you see when you take your eyes off the goal." "Just because you're paranoid doesn't mean that someone's not out to get you." And so on and so forth. And almost everyone we hired got the message and drank the Kool-Aid. Even the people who just wanted a "job" and not a career or to join a sacred crusade pretty much still worked their butts off.

But every so often, we'd hire someone who was just too healthy and well-adjusted to succeed among our tribe of crazies. We used to say that a relaxed man is not necessarily a better man. In one business, our internal motto was "let our sickness work for you". It turned out that it was important to let the other people see you sweat – not just the big deals – but the smallest details so they knew you cared. If you weren't just a little bit crazy about the work and the business, you were slightly suspect or worse.

I remember one special case where after we let someone go he wrote me a long letter and asked for a more complete explanation of why he didn't succeed with us. I decided to reply and ultimately what I ended up telling him is something that it's worth always keeping in mind when you sign up to be an entrepreneur. I wrote:

I'm sorry that complex issues like an individual's performance and work attitude get reduced to unfortunate shorthand phrases like "not hungry enough", "didn't want it", etc. in conversations with others who want to know "what happened?". We all know that work and relationships are far more complicated than a few pithy phrases. And we also know that, in their own mind, almost everyone wants to do a good job that they and others can be proud of. But here's the rub. Only a select few individuals are crazy enough (as we pretty much all are here) to subject themselves to the constant stress and heartache associated with starting and building new businesses. Our company is a very fast track run by a bunch of workaholic perfectionists. We all believe that that's what it takes to win against pretty fierce odds. And this is simply not the right place for everyone – especially people who want to have a family, outside interests and a normal life. I think it's very likely that you're simply too nice and too well-adjusted to work with the crazies around here and that's shame on us – not you. But it's the way things are. We wish you all the best.

Ultimately, all of these situations come down to the basic choice – you can make one person miserable for a period of time when they lose their job, or you can end up with a crappy company where everyone's miserable because you don't have the guts to do the right things for the business. And once you start to carry people along who aren't performing, you take a tremendous double hit – you pay the price for the poor performer's activities, but that's nothing compared to the real harm. As soon as you fail to consistently fire non-performers, you start to lose your best people and that's what kills the company.

To do this right, you have to build a differentiated system from the start that provides different levels of rewards, acknowledgments and compensation for different people throughout the business. And you need to move quickly and regularly to identify and remove the bad apples before they spoil the whole place.

STICK TO YOUR KNITTING

It turns out that the Three Musketeers had it half right. "All for one and one for all!" is a great strategy for assuring collaboration, teamwork and loyalty, but it can be a very dangerous approach in a start-up. This is because – notwithstanding the absolute best of intentions – it can lead to chaos in the kitchen with too many cooks and a whole lot of people trying to pitch in and "help out" who just end up being much more of a hindrance and a problem than if they simply minded their own business.

The fact is that, even if your business is short-handed and resource-constrained, you're not going to be well-served by people piling on to assist in areas where they don't have the skills, background or judgment to add value. Instead, they just get in the way or make things worse. Good intentions don't ever guarantee great results and, as the boss, you've got to politely tell these eager beavers to butt out. And you need to figure out a way to say "no thanks" without having them feel unappreciated, ignored or dismissed.

You don't want to crush their creativity or extinguish their enthusiasm, but you can't have your finance guys writing marketing copy (even in his alleged spare time) or your IT people trying to design your next product or service (unless perhaps you're in the IT business). And even then, if you are in the IT business, you still want your IT people taking care of their business and making sure that your servers and cloud connections don't blow up rather than suggesting new passionate, but sophisticated color schemes for your website.

Some skills are readily transferable and applicable across multiple disciplines, but too many people confuse energy, interest and even some skill with actual talent. I always loved it when I was making movies and people would dismiss a certain actor or actress and say that anyone could play that role. The truth is that the people up on the big screen are there for a reason – they have a certain electricity, attraction or whatever magic it is - and all the trying, practice, aspiration and desire won't ever help a million other wanna-bes duplicate their special presence. Stars are stars for a reason. They know that they can do one thing better than anyone else and the smartest ones do exactly that one thing and nothing else.

There's a reason that the people and companies that succeed in any line of business are those that focus their energy and resources and stick to their knitting. You need to be sure that both your company and your people have the same discipline. It's not even about what you actually say "yes" to and do, it's all about the many things that you have the guts to say "no" to and pass by even though they are terribly tempting.

This is all part of the process of what I'd call "getting real". It starts by admitting that democracy is not necessarily a virtue in all meetings; that not every idea is a good one or worth spending the group's time on; and that not everyone in the business is good at every part of the business or should be expected to be. And by the way, don't confuse bad ideas with bad intentions and don't forget that people can be terribly sincere and still have really stupid ideas.

It seems obvious, but I guarantee you that you'll find yourself stuck in these kinds of ultimately unproductive situations – especially as everyone in your company gets busier and busier – and the business continues to grow and expand. The basic nature of any start-up is a "let's get it done" attitude and, when things take longer than they should (with or without good reasons which may not be clear to everyone), there's a clear bias toward action – sometimes any action – and that's bad for everyone and really bad for the business because it encourages people who don't know what they're doing to roll up their sleeves and give themselves permission to try to do "something". Just because you can do something doesn't mean you should.

This is one of those cases where doing something really isn't necessarily better than doing nothing and waiting until the right people can get around to doing the thing that needs to get done and doing it the right way. It's hard for any entrepreneur to tell his people to hurry up and wait at the same time, but that's the right message. Stick to your knitting and mind your own part of the business.

FORGET ABOUT MOTIVATING
EMPLOYEES

I recently sent around a fairly direct (not to say harsh) memo to a number of our marketing folks which suggested that (a) being better prepared for certain meetings was a really good idea; and that (b) one great way to be better prepared was by making sure that they had seen and reviewed the videos and other materials which were going to be discussed in upcoming meetings before they got there – especially those specifically sent around by me.

Not only would this improve their participation and the value of their contributions to the meeting, but it would also avoid wasting my time and the time of many of the other attendees when we were forced to re-watch videos (which most of us had seen) so that we could all be on the same page during the meeting and have an intelligent and productive discussion. It seemed to me to be a fairly basic, straightforward and obvious request. Apparently, for at least some of the people, I wasn't being sensitive enough to how awfully busy they are and how hard it is for them to keep up with things. I guess that expecting people to do their jobs and telling them when you don't think they are has fallen out of fashion and is bad for morale. Shame on me.

But it got me thinking about motivation and about how too many of us have the whole motivation and incentive thing ass-backwards.

In the same way that too many people still think that education is about filling empty vessels (our kid's heads) with facts and figures rather than about igniting a passion for learning in them and creating environments that engage and excite them, way too many folks think that motivation is something that we do to other people. That it's the boss's job to be the team cheerleader and keep the troops pumped up. Basically, that this motivation business is an external process and a management tool which has to be learned and religiously applied to keep the wheels of the train from falling off.

But I think that's completely wrong. Real motivation comes entirely from within. People who pump themselves up stay pumped and succeed because passion and commitment and a true appreciation of why you're doing something and how it ultimately benefits you (and your family, etc.) are things that doesn't wear off or wear out and not some slogans, some incentives or some stupid party tricks that you read in some Dale Carnegie book. The simple truth is that there's no way to excite or motivate or inspire people that isn't grounded in their own perceived self-interest. And that's perfectly fine and the way it should be. No one's really against anyone else in business – they're just mainly interested in themselves and looking out for Number One.

So, if you're a leader and you want to effectively influence others, the process is actually pretty simple: you've got to talk about what they want (their future) and you've got to show them how to get it (the path) and then get out of their way and let nature take its course. They will take the information and – if they're engaged and excited about their prospects, their projects and their futures – they will create far more compelling and comprehensive reasons and justifications for working their butts off than you ever could because each of them knows exactly what's really important to them and you'd have to be a mind reader to even try to guess.

So forget about thinking that motivating your team is something you do to them and focus instead on doing things for them which removes obstacles, adds resources, clarifies directions and goals, and reduces friction so that they can see clearly what's ahead of them, how to get there and what's in it for them. The smart ones will be highly and authentically motivated all by themselves and the others will soon be working somewhere else.

TOO MUCH OF A GOOD THING
CAN BE BAD

Just about everything today is a double-edged sword. As much as we want passion from our people and a relentless commitment to the "cause", some moderation can be just as meaningful in many cases. We want a single-minded dedication to success, but surging mindlessly ahead can cause just as many serious setbacks as substantial scores over time. Speed doesn't help if you don't know where you're going. In fact, almost anything you do to excess comes back (in pretty short order) to bite you in the butt.

I see this all the time with young companies where the desire to be rapid and responsive makes everything into an emergency (however appropriate that may be) and - too many times — the rush of the urgent (and often immaterial) displaces the attention that needs to be paid to the really important things that will ultimately make a difference for the business. Not every situation needs to be turned into a crisis and not every customer issue or demand is critical and time-sensitive.

As often as not, giving a little time and a little more thought to a measured and smart response to a given situation pays larger dividends in the long run (for you and the customer) than taking a knee-jerk swat at the problem and hoping for the best. So, in certain circumstances, you can actually be too responsive, too reactive, too eager, and too quick for your own good.

But, in all my years of thinking about these things, I never really thought you could be "too" focused. I've said and believed for years that an obsessive focus on a few critical parts of your business was probably the most important discipline that you needed to master in order to succeed. Turns out I was wrong and you can be "too" anything if you're not careful.

My thought always was to be constantly mobilizing "all the wood behind a single arrowhead" so that you could maximize the force and impact of your activities. This is how you avoided being "a mile wide and an inch deep" in your business and essentially diluting your results (or doing a crappy job) on a lot of different things.

Many years ago, the Japanese figured this out in a process that they called the "hard drill" where they knew that they couldn't take on multiple industries because they were too time and resource constrained so they would identify a single industry (think about how they took over the copier business) and then deeply and directly attack that marketplace rather than wasting their efforts on several industries and not making a dent anywhere.

But, these days, there are new critical considerations – principally due to the prospect of aggressive and rapid disruptive innovation which now threatens every market. Because of the low cost of competing and the ease of market entry; because of the speed of change and its discontinuous rather than evolutionary nature; and because businesses are facing both traditional and non-traditional global competitors, the strategy of bearing down and looking straight ahead turns out to risk putting you and your business at a competitive information disadvantage because you literally may not see the competition and the problems coming.

Not only are many of the most serious threats likely to arise from way down the food chain; others are just as likely to jump into your market from adjacent and seemingly tangential sectors where various technical, legal or geographical barriers previously precluded such actions. In the old days, the typical process of competitive responses was a five step progression:

1. Ignore

2. Ridicule

3. Attack

4. Copy

5. Steal

But, if you aren't on the lookout and don't see these guys coming, they're likely to roll right over you before you know what happened. We may have a new Man of Steel these days, but our domestic steel industry was completely destroyed by quick, cheap foreign steel producers who started at the very bottom of the market creating things that no one else even wanted to make and then quickly moved up from that base to take over the entire business.

The bottom line: you've got to pay attention not only to the business you have and the competition that you can see, but also – and maybe even more critically – you've got to keep a sharp eye out for the guys lurking just over the hill who are getting ready to eat your lunch if you're not on the ball. As the saying goes, just because you're paranoid doesn't mean that someone isn't out to get you.

WIKI-WORK: FREE TO BE
WHERE I WANT

I'm convinced that if, by virtue of someone's magic wand, we instantly had freely-transferable (and truly portable) and reasonably-priced insurance coverage for everyone (regardless of prior conditions and other similar insurance company scams and dodges) who was presently gainfully employed in the United States, we would instantly see two amazing occurrences: (1) a GIGANTIC movement to new jobs, new start-up businesses and other new and exciting opportunities by millions of employees who are presently trapped in horrible, useless and unproductive jobs because they (and their families) are prisoners and/or hostages of their existing insurance coverage and their prior medical histories; and (2) an equally ENORMOUS boost in overall growth and productivity as well as in our nation's GNP as the talents, energies and skills of these insurance "slaves" were suddenly freed up and applied to valuable, innovative and exciting new ventures of every size and shape.

There's a great deal of conversation these days about why productivity increases and technology advancements are no longer resulting in improved median income levels for huge segments of the population and why only a precious few people and businesses keep getting richer and richer as a result of these drivers. It turns out that for many years and until very recently even the best economists were misled by the purely coincidental parallel movements of productivity improvements, job growth and increases in median income. It turns out that there's no necessary connection and that productivity or technology improvements don't have to necessarily help or financially benefit the vast majority of us. Life still isn't fair or – as that great old William Gibson saying goes – you might say "the future is already here – it's just not very evenly distributed".

Another huge time sink is the constant conversations about skills gaps and the need to retrain zillions of workers to equip them for 21st century jobs. I don't feel that these concerns are misplaced; it's just that - when entrepreneurs look at issues like these rather than bureaucrats and politicians – we focus on the lowest hanging fruit and the solutions that can give us immediate results and the most bang for our bucks. The real name of the game is to overcome the horrible resource displacement that's a product of our stupid politicians and our restrictive and anti-competitive laws and policies and of the antiquated ideas about insurance coverage, education, etc. that prevent the kinds of real changes and simple solutions that could make quick and comprehensive contributions to our overall economy and to the economic well-being of millions.

I've said my piece about insurance, but consider that the entire world can access educational videos now anywhere and anytime except in one place – in our school classrooms – where state restrictions driven by teacher union lobbyists prevent even smart and forward-looking teachers – from using these "free" resources in their classrooms to provide their students with the "best of breed" kinds of instruction that are now available. As hard as this is to believe, in states like Illinois, "virtual" instruction has to be delivered by an Illinois state-certified instructor. Interstate commerce – forget about it. Globalization – don't bring that stuff in my house. And as to the morons who are our political representatives – all I can say is that: "if horses could vote, there would never have been cars".

The truth is that we've got plenty of talent, plenty of skills and plenty of people in this country right now – but huge numbers of workers are in the wrong places doing the wrong jobs – and all because we haven't figured out two crucial things: how to increase their mobility so they can move to better positions and better paying jobs (portable insurance for a starter) and, in the case of the millions of place-bound and otherwise location-challenged workers - how to bring the jobs to them which I call for ease of reference Wiki-Work (web-distributed, massive scale, collaborative work executed in bits and pieces) to effectively recapture millions of man hours of lost time and productive effort.

The models and examples are there. The solutions are fairly obvious and not costly. There are entrepreneurs just waiting in the wings all over the world to jump on these problems. The question is when and whether we have the will and the courage to make the changes that will make a better world for generations to come.

THE 5 A'S OF EFFECTIVE OUTSOURCING

If you're a smart and strategic entrepreneur running a start-up today, you should be spending part of your time trying to pare your business down so that you can focus your people and resources on doing just those things that you're terrific at (or going to be terrific at) and – at the same time – trying to shed everything that doesn't really add value to the process. If something you're spending time and money on isn't building an advantage for you and helping your business to create one or more sustainable competitive edges, you should be doing something else. Think of it as outsourcing uber alles – you need to bag everything you can't do a lot better than a million other people because just doing things as well as the next guy won't cut it anymore. Average is over.

In the not so old days, people used to look critically at businesses that were somewhat "virtual" and often accuse them of being composed mainly of "smoke and mirrors" – politely suggesting that these enterprises were really scams because there wasn't an obvious "there" there. Essentially, there weren't enough concrete, computers and other serious capital expenditures to give prospective investors or customers comfort that the business was secure, solid and real. Today, most of those same folks would call you "stupid" if you were buying and building your own servers; handling your own HR and accounting; and fundamentally failing to farm out every other function that you didn't need to staff and run yourself because it was core to your company and central to your strategy.

But selecting the right vendor/partner for the various services you are seeking to outsource isn't as easy as you might imagine because everybody lies. Everyone tells you what you want to hear and virtually everyone will basically say that they can do anything that you need done. So, I've developed a pretty straightforward checklist and I've found that – even if you don't always get the straight scoop and a full answer – by the time you've worked your way through these questions, you'll have a gut feeling as to whether this is someone that you want to be in business with and frankly that's about the best that you can do in a case like this. You won't be an entrepreneur if you didn't go with your gut more often than not anyway, but here at least you'll have a framework to help make sure that you cover the basic bases and that you don't go off half-cocked just to get the process over so you can get back to your more important business. Actually, getting these selections right is VERY important business and critically important to your business as well. So don't sell it short and don't try to rush it – it's worth the taking the time to do it right the first time so that you don't end off in a few weeks or months doing it all over again.

I call these things the 5 A's although in this age of everything inflation, you'll see that there're more like a dozen A's in the mix. Some are more objective criteria than others and those you can get some help answering by the standard methods. As an example, it actually does make sense to do some customer and reference checks before you sign on the dotted line. Others are impressions and feelings that you should try to elicit in the course of your conversations. And speaking of conversations, get yourself in front of the people who run the business – not the salesmen who sell business for them. It's those guys that you want to be looking at – eyeball to eyeball – when you're trying to decide if they'll go the extra mile and really look after your interests and your business when things get bumpy – as they always do at some point. If the right people are willing to show up and make the right kinds of commitments and assurances, and if you believe them, then you've done about the best job that you can.

So here's my short list of A's.

(A1) Ability and (Actual) Accomplishments

This one is pretty easy and referenceable. You need to make sure that they've actually done (and done well) the particular work you're asking them to do. Law firms, as an example, are notorious for saying they can do anything, but you really don't want anybody "learning" how to do something on your dime. You want the people who have done it before - not the ones who watched - or the ones who think they can do it. This is stuff you can (and definitely should) check out with their existing clients and customers. And while you're at it make sure they have the resources and the capacity to take your additional business on and to handle it from the "get-go" - not grow into it and try to add people to support it over time.

(A2) Anal and Accountable

This one's about personalities and whether they're a "fit" for you and the way you do business. Find a place that takes things personally and you're most likely to find some folks who are just as anal and driven as you are about how things should be done. By the way, these people may sometimes drive you crazy – but in a good way. Just expect some strongly expressed opinions and you'll do fine. There's always a right way to do things - you've just got to find folks who care about doing things that way and who are willing to commit the time, people and other resources necessary to do the job that way each and every time. This is the culture you want in your own company and it's essential that the people and firms helping to support you share the same work ethic and "take no prisoners" attitude. Otherwise, you set up a second class of service and your people start wasting their own time and energy pointing fingers and complaining about the work that the outsourcers aren't getting done on time and on the money.

(A3) Aggressive and Assertive

In building your external team, you want people who are leaders in their own markets – people leaning forward and into the game, not coasting or resting on their laurels. These people don't come cheap, but they're worth the investment. You will never save your way to any success worth securing – spend the money and do things right the first time. These people also tend to be fast and aggressive and they will challenge you to move quickly yourself as well. And - God forbid - they agree with everything you suggest or propose. There are only two scenarios in the real world where this kind of obsequies agreement and compliance occurs: (a) when two people consistently agree on everything, one of them is excess baggage at best and should be gone; and (b) when two people agree on everything, it turns out that one of them isn't engaged or listening and that's as bad for your business as the guy who bends over at every opportunity. Good people ask hard, direct questions and won't be pushed aside or put off. If you do that too often, they'll just pick up and leave.

(A4) Adaptable and Ambidextrous

We live in a world where's there's no "business as usual" left anywhere and you need to be sure that the partners you're picking are committed to changing with the times and changing all the time because the stark choices today are: change or die. Some deaths will be abrupt and some will be painfully slow, but you can be sure that people trying to pitch yesterday's solutions and ways of doing business to growing companies trying to address tomorrow's problems and the new challenges that arise every day are basically the walking dead and doomed. In addition to just the volume of sheer change that needs to be addressed, there's a related concern which is equally crucial. Vendors who still believe that one size of anything fits everything or that one approach or solution automatically scales and applies to most of their customers aren't people you want to be in business with because that's another sure formula for failure. Everything today needs to be customized and hyper-personalized to suit the precise and very exacting needs of each customer. Your suppliers need to be flexible enough to go in multiple directions at the same time (offering competing, conflicting and contradictory solutions to different parties) and to understand that – with today's rates of change – that what worked well for you yesterday might just be a major problem for you today and tomorrow for sure. It won't be easy for them to track and manage all these variables (and they would much prefer not to have to try), but if they don't learn to adapt their products and services along multiple and alternative vectors, they won't be of much help to you and they won't be around themselves much longer.

(A5) Always Additive

I don't like people who come to play – I like people who play to win. There's always a better, cheaper, faster or more efficient way to do things and I'm sorry to say that you personally aren't going to have the time, the bandwidth or even the ability to figure everything out yourself so you need to surround yourself with teams of people who are domain experts (in each of their areas) and count on them to contribute new ideas, approaches and solutions that will move your business forward. People who are there just to save you a dollar (or to make themselves a dollar) aren't going to be the ones to make a major difference for you. People who can add to the equation and keep raising the bar are force multipliers and you need to get them on-board and then get out of their way. Remember that customer expectations across the board are progressive – if you're not pushing the ball forward, you're losing ground to someone.

And, by the way, since every business is always "selling" themselves (and their products and services) to someone, you might take a few minutes to ask yourself how well your partners, vendors, customers, suppliers, and employees would say that your own company satisfies the 5 A's in dealing with them. Looking in the mirror isn't always a narcissistic exercise – sometimes it's a harsh and necessary evil – and a very effective way to see the most accurate reflection of how the outside world sees your business.

ALWAYS BE READY TO BAIL OR BOLT

In today's hyper-competitive marketplace, the most sought-after and desirable employees are the ones whose bags are always packed – not because they are disloyal or disinterested – but because they recognize that "up or out" is the way of the world today.

If you're not ready, willing and able to step forward and seize the next best opportunity – within or outside of your own company – then you'll discover pretty quickly that the people making the decisions and the key personnel selections will start to look right past you when the best opportunities are on the table.

They need people who will jump at the chance to move across the country, take on new and uncertain challenges without the slightest qualms, and – most of all – who understand that there are no guarantees of comfort, security or success these days – just the guarantee that anyone standing still (or "just" doing their job) will be blown away by the people who are doing a whole lot more and who make their interest, aptitude and attitude known.

The world today is divided into targets and gunslingers. Hot shots and has-beens (regardless of your age). Everyone is in someone else's sights and plenty of people are gunning for your position. That's why it's a good idea to keep your boots by the side of your bed – just like the firemen do.

And it's also important to remember that it's not so much a case of taking you for granted (although there are certainly elements of that) or any dissatisfaction with your current performance – it's much more about attitude and the feeling on management's part that you're not likely to be the person to take the business to the next level – regardless of the level that you're at and regardless of how important the particular assignment is.

If it's not abundantly clear that you want it (whatever the "it" happens to be) a lot more than the next twelve guys and that you're prepared to make the commitment and the sacrifices necessary to see things through and get the new job done and done well and on time and on budget, then it's very easy today for the company to find someone else who's a better bet.

So what can you do to increase your favorable odds and your visibility without overstepping the bounds of propriety or pissing off your peers? Here are a few things you can do now to get ready to be great.

(1) Sharpen Your Sights and Step Up Your Skills

It helps a whole lot to know specifically what you're shooting for. Chasing too many rabbits usually results in ending up empty handed. Set a goal, make a plan, and go for it. And while you're waiting for good things to happen, make sure you're constantly honing and updating your skill sets, adding new tools and technologies to your war chest, and learning all the while from anyone and everyone willing to share with you. Good listeners are in terribly short supply and you'd be amazed at how much valuable information people will part with if they know you're interested and that they're appreciated. Soak it all up – lifetime learners are superb sponges – and that's a good thing.

(2) Streamline Your Story and Skinny Down Your Price Tag

It's actually quite possible to be too much of a good thing in the job market and to be perceived as over-qualified for a new position that you'd absolutely kill for. It's nice to be subtle and to stay above the fray, but that's not what people are looking for today. They want people who want it and want it bad and who aren't afraid or ashamed to admit it. Those who never ask rarely, if ever, get what they want. Most of the things in life that just drop into your lap don't really belong there, aren't really worth that much, and generally result in a mess of one kind or another.

Don't try to be so delicate or oblique that your message and your interest get lost in the process. You want to be sure that, when the time and circumstances are right, you're in the game and on the short list and that you make your interest, appetite and aptitude for the new position known to all concerned. Don't ever assume that anyone besides you knows what's best or just right for you and shame on you if you don't tell them.

And, if you're not careful, you can also easily price yourself out of a new opportunity before you even get a chance to have a conversation with the people doing the search. You never really want to negotiate against yourself, but it's very important to make sure that the folks around you (and above you) know that money isn't the thing that matters the most to you.

Money is just the way that people without talent try to keep score. Doing important work; doing it exceptionally well; and getting the right, timely results is what ultimately counts and where the real satisfaction in your work will be found. Making it critical that you get a bump in your current compensation into the prime consideration in your ongoing search for your next career move is a major mistake that is most likely to lead to a very rocky road going forward. Prove yourself first – it always pays off in the long run.

(3) Scrap Your Sidekicks (Entourage) and Bag Your Baggage

Package deals may work great for travel agents and casinos, but they don't help in the hiring process. In fact, they're a drag and a major hindrance. People who try to bring too much baggage with them don't get a shot at the brass ring. You need to worry about yourself – first and foremost – and then, once you've made it over the hurdles and beyond the barricades, you can always reach back for your buddies. But, in the beginning, the old, time-tested rule still applies: he travels fastest and furthest who travels alone. It may be a lonely journey at first, but at least it's not crowded.

And try also to lose as many of the other typical kinds of impediments as possible if you really want to make a successful move. As sad as this is to say, the fact is that the more integrated into and tightly bound you are to your community and your surroundings and your outside activities, the less likely you are to make it onto many a short list. There's nothing wrong with this (from a social and family standpoint it's probably a very good thing), but you should understand that there's an embedded choice that it represents unless you actively signal and communicate otherwise which will have serious career consequences.

We're in a global race these days and you've got to be willing to get up and go where the action is whenever you're asked. And - make no mistake – you will rarely be asked twice because there's a long line right behind you of folks ready, willing and able to step right over you and into those new, bigger shoes if you hesitate in the least. They might be younger, unmarried, childless, not house or condo bound, etc. and they are raring to go.

So, while it may be a conscious decision and the right choice for you and your family, just be aware that family and community ties are just that – "ties" that can restrict and limit your chances to move onward and upward – whether anyone ever admits that to you or not.

YOU CAN ALWAYS GO BACK.
(BETTER)

I think an end is in sight. That giant sucking sound which accompanied the annual flood of all the smartest quants, developers and systems engineers being swept up and into the giant banks, hedge funds, VC/PE firms and other financial institutions (never to be seen again) may finally be quieting down.

More and more talented programmers and engineers are bailing out – looking for better, not necessarily bigger – and leaving the "friendly confines" and the comfort of their current positions to look for new opportunities. And "confines" they really were. Turns out that, once you actually got into that tantalizing temple of men and money, you'd quickly discover that at the end of the day – however much money you were making and however well-appointed your digs were – you were still a troll in the tunnel. And it wasn't anyone's idea of the Tunnel of Love.

And, of course, the most ironic aspect of the situation is that the new attitudes and behaviors which are driving these alternative occupational choices are more apparent and more consistently present these days in many an employment calculation even though the long economic drought is finally beginning to abate. Big bonuses are back and sadly it's still way too much "business as usual" on Wall Street. You'd think nothing ever blew up and, of course, since no one with any true culpability was ever punished, it's like the whole deal happened to some other guys and we all just read about it in the papers. And, for sure, since this is a culture that never learns its lessons, you can expect a whole lot more of the same down the line.

So it's a lot more "show me the door" than "show me the money" these days. And really, for the good guys, the job was never about the money anyway – it was always about the work and not about the perks. It had much more to do with the idea of and the freedom to tackle the really challenging problems which were fundamentally changing the way in which the world's financial markets worked.

And it's not like we've solved all those issues; it's just that today is all about tweaks and tweaking (just like twerking) is nothing to write home about or brag about to your hacking buddies. It's the difference between inventing the Model T, on the one hand, and worrying about how long the fins and tail lights should be on this year's model, on the other.

So the smartest guys aren't locked-in, laser-focused, heads down and grinding out new code any more. The truth is that they're realizing that they're not chained to their desks and they're heads up and heading for the door in droves. So, if the shoe fits you, you need to start thinking about the same things if you don't want to be left behind in the new digital Gold Rush. Get going, get out there while the getting is good, and make sure you get yours.

Now I know that this is an easier thing to say than it is to do for many people and that most developers and engineers are surprisingly conservative whether they'd admit it or not. Structure and stability is a goal in their code and a major virtue in their lives as well. And that's why I'm going to share a little secret with all of you which should make the process a lot simpler, safer and more comfortable.

Here's the secret: You Can Always Go Back. (Better)

Now what exactly does that mean? It's really simple. If you're not an asshole when you leave (and you don't leave anyone in the lurch), they'll always take you back in a heartbeat if things don't work out better for you out there in the "real" world.

And just why would they do that? Because on the round trip, you'll be a better trained, more experienced, and especially more up-to-date candidate for the position. The fact is that everyone gets stale and everyone gets a little lazy. So if you've been in a job for years and you're working with the same code base and working on variations and tweaks of the same problem set, you're just not likely to also be the one guy in a thousand who spends his weekends making sure that he's current on everything new that happening. And you're also not likely to be the guy who wakes up one morning with a ridiculous and counter-intuitive approach to handling some problem that's been staring your whole team in the face for months or years. Radical change and disruptive innovation come from the outside of organizations, not from the people in charge or the one's maintaining the status quo.

So, instead of being a scarlet letter or something to be ashamed of (as if you were disloyal and abandoned ship), the fact that you joined a start-up trying to change the world or spent a year or two learning a new set of mobile tools or some crazy new e-commerce platform isn't a bad thing – it's actually a career-booster, even at your old place of employment. I've seen it happen a million times already – if you're good and newly- gung ho to jump back in, only someone who's a complete management moron would hold a grunge and bar the door back in. If they're smart, they'll ask you if you've stumbled across 3 more guys who also want to join up and also have new skills, new strengths, and a new outlook on how to approach the key issues. As long as they're not bitter and happy to have you back; you're actually in a better position and a better hire than anyone else they could find because you know the ropes and the mess of legacy spaghetti that they call their code.

So what are you waiting for? There's a big wide world out there waiting for you to rattle a few cages and make some critical, game-changing changes. And you can do it. And, worst case, you can always come back. Better.

DON'T GUESS, ASK

I don't mind people who are easily or regularly confused. At least they're thinking and, frankly, confusion is a higher state of knowledge than ignorance. And, most of the time, I don't even mind blissful ignorance. A great deal of the early enthusiasm in building a business comes from a combination of ignorance, bad information and wilful self-delusion and - as often as not – it helps you get over a bunch of those early humps.

And the even better news is that, with some time and some education, ignorance is basically curable. That's why, having spent the last decade or so building and rebuilding colleges, I've always liked the old expression: "if you think education is expensive, try ignorance". Although I wouldn't say that the most important education for an entrepreneur is ever found in the classroom – it's always found in the streets and in the trial-and-error process. Really effective education, for better or worse, takes you slowly from cocky ignorance to miserable uncertainty because real knowledge is essentially discovering and acknowledging the extent of your ignorance (notwithstanding whatever crazy conjugations Donald Rumsfeld may have come up with) and then moving forward to fill those gaps.

Ignorance really is a big part of the start-up game and, in some cases, it's almost a competitive advantage not to understand or appreciate just how tough, costly and long the process of building something new and important can really be. I always say that, if we entrepreneurs knew how hard the journey was going to be, we might not have started down the path in the first place. And, ultimately, the truth is that ignorance won't necessarily kill you or your business; it's just guaranteed to make you sweat a lot. So I'm OK with some ignorance. But what I really can't stand is ignorance combined with arrogance and I see way too much of this around me these days. And there's nothing more frightening than arrogant ignorance in action.

I'm sure that you've experienced these things as well and there are many forms of the problem, but I want to focus on a single instance which, and this may just be my painful past experiences talking, I think has everything to do with your age. Those of us of a certain grand old age were raised with a lot of rules and one of the most fundamental rules of all was that you asked permission before (not after) you did something.

Now I know all about it supposedly being so much better in our crazy and aggressive start-up culture to just rush straight ahead and try to get a jump on things and then beg for forgiveness afterwards (instead of asking for permission) – and believe me, I've been there and done that a bunch of times. But there was a pretty critical distinction - I might have often rushed ahead without permission, but I leaped without as much information as I could possibly gather before I moved an inch.

And, here's the bottom line: the way you get the information that you need is very, very simple. You don't guess, you ask. As hard as it is to believe, this seems like a foreign concept to an amazing number of young entrepreneurs that we deal with every day. If you ask the right people for the required information and/or direction, the odds of your going off half-cocked and being dead wrong are virtually zero. So why wouldn't anyone with a brain take a minute, catch their breath and ask before they acted?

I think that the problem is arrogance. They're too smart for their own good and too lazy at the same time. This is the triumph of hubris over homework. "I don't have to ask – I'll just jump and, if I mess things up, so be it. Someone else can clean up my mess". And when the mistakes do happen and you ask them why they didn't spend the marginal few minutes to get the goods and get things done right (the first time), they hide behind these silly platitudes from B school. I call this ignorance acting in the name of initiative. They'll say things like: "I thought you wanted me to think for myself" or "I was just taking the initiative" when the truth really is that they were being arrogant and assumptive and, worst of all, too lazy and/or too proud to do the preparation and ask for the assistance that they needed to do the right thing.

I don't see this going away any time soon, but it's important as a leader and a manager (especially in a young company where communication is so critical) to make it; (1) more than O.K. for anyone to ask questions (not stupid or embarrassing) and to make it (2) very, very clear that everyone needs to be sure that they have all the information available before they act and that (3) they understand that there's no upside in guessing what anyone wants or expects or assuming that they know what the right actions are through some process of divine inspiration.

It couldn't be easier. Don't guess, ask.

WALLFLOWERS, BAGGAGE AND "BITCHES"

I was recently part of an all-male ARA panel discussion (moderated by Sandee Kastrul from i.c. stars) and held at 1871 in front of another 250 women to discuss The Male Perspective on Women in Technology. I thought that it was a very enlightening session for all of us and - after the necessary disclaimers about why any woman would ever care what any men thought about this subject - and why there weren't any women on the panel - we got down to a mostly serious discussion (with a few laughs about men who cry) talking about what could be done to help improve the current – pretty depressing – percentages of women in the technology sector. Bob Miano, CEO of Harvey Nash, said in his comments that the numbers have remained flat and pretty constant for the last several years according to their annual surveys.

The panel discussion was prefaced by a short keynote talk by Brenna Berman, the CIO for the City of Chicago, and she noted (essentially on the issue of who cares what the guys think) that some of her most valuable mentors over the years had been men who had assisted and supported her progress throughout her career so she certainly believed that their thoughts and concerns were, in fact, pretty relevant. I felt she handled this touchy question very well and that her opening comment was a helpful and instructive observation which cleared the modestly tense air a bit before our discussion started.

Of course, not everything was roses after that. In the blogs following the event, she was quoted (I'm assuming accurately) as saying that she thought, on occasion, that the male panelists were giving answers that didn't fit the questions and that it would have been interesting to see (at the same time and in the same context) how women panelists might have answered those precise questions. For my part, I thought that - across the board – the male panelists gave straight and honest answers to the best of their abilities and avoided any kind of politically correct crap, but, of course, this is what makes horse races. And, as someone else noted, we were a group of guys who fundamentally believed that we were on the right side of this issue anyway and so I doubt that we were necessarily full-fledged members of the target population whose mindsets needed to be changed or expanded. I said in my opening comments that I've been gender-blind in my hiring decisions and team compositions for more than 40 years and that I was plenty proud of the fact that every business I've built had women as part of the senior management from the beginning.

In any event, I came away with a couple of thoughts and pieces of advice that I would share especially with all the young women in my various ventures who are just getting started in the business world or in the world of building their own businesses. These were mainly drawn from the comments of the other panelists although I will take credit for eventually providing a pretty good answer to the main "curve ball" question of the night even though I ducked it when it was first asked by saying that I had promised my team in writing that I wouldn't answer that particular inquiry.

(1) Wallflowers Aren't Really Welcome

Roger Liew, the CTO of Orbitz, made a very important point which – in my writings – I've usually short-handed by saying either that "feasibility will compromise you soon enough" or "don't let other people's fears or limitations hold you back". There are always plenty of people willing to tell you why you can't do something and it's very important that you yourself not be one of them. Roger had his own very interesting experiences about assigning women on his team certain high-visibility and important projects and then having to convince them (not to say "beg them") to step up and take on the job. His point was that no guy would ever say he wasn't up to the task (whatever the task was) and neither should any woman especially because they should know that their boss or manager wouldn't have asked them to take the job if he or she had any doubts in their ability to get it done and done well. You need to know that in any business everyone "wings it" from time to time and the key to success is simply that some people do it much more confidently than others. So don't be afraid to step forward when you next have the chance and don't ever sell yourself short. You'll always miss 100% of the shots you don't take.

(2) Leave the Baggage in the Lobby

Matt Hancock, Executive Director of the Chicago Tech Academy High School, said that, if he had only one piece of advice for young women entering the tech world, it would be to forget all the "expert" advice and all the "Dos and Don't" about how to act in the workforce and just leap right in and go with the flow. He called this "dropping all the baggage" and showing up as you are. If you let your contributions and actions speak for you and use the skills that you uniquely possess, you can make a real impact and a difference. I'd say it slightly differently, but the point is the same: all the good advice, pre-game coaching and helpful hints in the world won't ultimately make you a better you. Everyone's an expert who doesn't have to do these things themselves. Only you can make these things happen for yourself and it helps a lot to be sure that you don't get in your own way while you are doing just that.

(3) Being Passionate Isn't a Bad Thing

The closing question of the night was the closest thing to a curve ball and dealt with a very touchy area. The question was: "How do you suggest coming across confident without being perceived as a "Bitch" or overly aggressive?" I'm sure that there are a number of good hints or suggestions in the literature on this subject, but I thought that the right approach wasn't to try to outline rules of behavior or language suggestions which would have just amounted to piling on more of Matt's "baggage" (see above). The truth is and the best answer (for me at least) is that you need to change the conversation and the lens that you're looking through.

Aggression is so weighted and ugly a word that I can't think of any context in which we would truly value it (except maybe in pro sports where we reward violent actions by morons already being driven mad by steroids) and so we need to put that particular word aside and have a smarter and more productive discussion. Talking about a fierce passion to succeed, on the other hand; or about an uncompromising commitment to a cause or a business; and/or discussing a "take no prisoners" attitude are all positions and postures that we heartily endorse and, in fact, hope to emulate in our own behavior. Passion is just the flip (and far more attractive) side of aggression and that's how we should answer the question. The ones who want it the most and care the most are the ones who make things happen.

Passion is what moves mountains and makes the world move forward. Passion and unflinching optimism are force multipliers. There's never enough to go around because these qualities are always in short supply. So, the bottom line is self-evident. It's short-sighted and stupid to discourage anyone's (males or females) energy and enthusiasm and it's long past time that we got over the rhetoric and the pointless characterizations and started focusing our efforts and energies on who can best help us make a difference in the marketplace and create real results.

IGNORANCE ISN'T BLISS ANYMORE - IT'S IMMINENT OBLIVION

Not exactly sure what "oblivion" means? Well, take a minute and look it up. And, in a way, that's precisely my point. Some of you will already know what it means; some of you will think you know (Goethe called this frightening phenomena: "ignorance in action", but it's actually a case of ignorance begetting inaction); some of you will take the time to look it up and be the better for it; some of you just won't care (shame on you); and most of you will say (hopefully to yourselves) that you just don't have the time.

But, of course, you do. Here's a tip about time: if you really want to do something, you'll find the time and a way to do it. If you don't, you'll find an excuse. The fact is that - even in our frantic and time-constrained world — we have all the time that we need (or we can make the time) for the things that we are actually interested in. And if you're not interested in life-long learning and in constantly trying to make yourself smarter and better-informed, you're not gonna be of much value to anyone (including yourself) and you certainly won't be able to compete effectively in the new knowledge economy. And this isn't just an attitude that you'll need; it needs to be a prominent part of your company's culture as well unless you also want your company to be an afterthought or yesterday's news.

Today, one of the greatest obstacles to progress isn't ignorance; it's the illusion of knowledge which – as often as not – is bound up in our arrogance and our reluctance to admit that we may not know it all. Real knowledge today is as much about knowing the extent of your ignorance (what you don't know) as it is about what you actually do know. Now don't get me wrong. I'm not trying to do some rhetorical Rumsfeld rap here – I'm just sayin'. And, unlike Rummy, I think there's good news on the horizon and a pretty simple solution to the problem.

Ignorance fortunately is curable; stupidity sadly is forever. We can't save most folks from their own stupidity or laziness, but I'm hopeful that we can help you get everyone in your business focused on getting better and smarter all the time with a simple turn of a phrase. Because even if ignorance doesn't kill you; it's certainly gonna make you sweat a lot more than you need to. So here's a simple suggestion on how to change the conversation and the culture in a few words.

The next time anyone anywhere says "I don't know", tell them that that phrase no longer means "they lack knowledge"; it just means that they're lazy because they didn't take the time to find out. DON'T KNOW = DIDN'T LOOK. Because the answers to just about anything we need to know today are out there; we just need to go find them. And to paraphrase Yoda: it's not about "trying" half-heartedly to find the information; it's about doing it with a vengeance. And, to remain competitive in today's economy, your team needs to know where to look and how to find the right answers fast. Because you can be sure that someone else is right behind you looking over your shoulder for the same advantage.

Sometimes it's a really short journey. It's not even about automatically searching the web. In many cases, you just need to do a better job of knowing what's going on in your own shop. I call this the "If P & G only knew what P & G knows" syndrome and it's applicable to every business – large and small. The answers, my friends, aren't always in the stars; sometimes they're in ourselves. In other cases, even a simple web search will provide more relevant and actionable information than you can imagine and more real value as well. It's not always that easy – so tenacity and perseverance matter as well – but the rewards for persistence are clear.

But your people have to have the intention, the inclination, and your permission to look – a bias toward investigation and learning – and not the self-satisfied and smug attitude that they already know everything worth knowing. Education isn't cheap; but ignorance is beyond costly. I recommend getting a t-shirt for the ones who just refuse to get with the program (while they're packing their bags) which says: "I DON'T KNOW AND I'M TOO LAZY TO GO FIND OUT". Not knowing is a sin; not caring about not knowing is grounds for termination.

The fact is that, except for your lawn sprinkling system, I'm afraid that there's nothing left in our world that can operate on the "set it and forget it" principle which made life so easy for so many people in the past. The vast amount of data; the prospect of constant feedback and trend information; and the ability to change the behavior of our customers in real time are all raising the need to be (a) on the case, (b) in the know, (c) all the time. Not knowing isn't even a bad excuse anymore; it's a death sentence for your business.

WHERE IS IT WRITTEN?

Where is it written that a 26 year-old is entitled to a 6-figure salary? The rampant grade inflation at our colleges and universities where everyone's apparently an "A" student and where grading on a curve is just for old-fashioned curmudgeons like me is nothing compared to the ego and compensation inflation that's also going on all around us. Salaries always spike when there's tons of easy money chasing deals, but today it seems like the finances of too many startups are entirely out of whack with both reality and with their own wherewithal.

We used to believe that the cash and other compensation which you earned were reasonably correlated to the contributions that you made to the business. "Made" in the past tense – not those you were hoping or expected to make in the future. But today, recent graduates and new employees (especially in tech businesses) want to be paid on the come and - in addition to being unbecoming and overreaching – these expectations are choking a lot of young businesses because it would appear that almost no one in management knows how to say "No" anymore. In fact, I'm not sure that any of these young CEOs really want to say "No" (and here's another change from the past) because the salaries being paid to the people working for them are a pretty good justification for the amount of their own compensation as well. So no one really has the guts or the motivation to slay the Golden Goose until it's too late.

I'm afraid that, if we don't take some time to review the situation and maybe re-set some of the benchmarks, we're going to see a lot more businesses abruptly hitting the wall when the cash runs out before there's any real traction for the business and before the results start to show. You can shift your strategy and pivot like crazy if you've got the funds to stay in the game, but when you run out of cash, they send you to the showers and then straight home with your tail between your legs.

What's interesting to me is that this problem is pretty much restricted to the new young tech companies rather than the established Silicon Valley technology businesses that have been in the game for many years. In part, this situation is probably because a great deal of what used to consume a significant part of early-stage funds (capital expenditures, connectivity costs, etc.) are really no longer major components of getting a new business off the ground. So there's more theoretically "free" cash to spend on disproportionate comp packages for the management and key technical employees.

In fact, the big tech guys not only understood the salary and comp problems; they appear to have adopted an entire – basically illegal - plan to deal with it. That hasn't worked out too well for them at the moment, but you can't blame them for trying. At least they were a lot smarter than the legal profession which basically blew itself up (and killed a number of major firms) by engaging in an insane annual competition to see which firms could pay the largest starting salaries to their newest associates. Year after year for no good reason they would pay newbies tens of thousands of dollars more than their existing employees and brag about it to boot. I'm sure that the stupidity of this competitive process wasn't lost on the senior management at Apple, Google, etc. An interesting aside is that one of the only companies not accused of participating in this comp-fixing scheme was Facebook which was also run by the youngest guy on the block.

In any event, and however they came to the realization that some collusion was in their aggregate best interests, we're all reading these days about the latest class action lawsuits asserting that certain executives at the biggest tech firms on the West Coast got together and agreed not to poach talent from each other by starting bidding wars for engineers and other workers with specialized technical skills. They allegedly had an aggressive and quite overt enforcement policy among the major firms and an ongoing and active involvement from the most senior managers in the whole process. Most recently, the judge rejected a major settlement offer by the leading firms (about $325 million) saying that she thought it wasn't enough money for the damage done to the hundreds or thousands of employees who got screwed.

I'm not sure how the litigation will turn out for the parties (I know the lawyers will make a bundle), but I'm certain that I can understand some of the underlying motivations (not, of course, the morality or legality) of most of these guys. It's hard enough to get great talent and almost impossible in the hyper-competitive and completely immoral world of the Valley to hang on to your best people because everyone is basically chasing the same players and most of those players are chasing the next "big bucks" offer. Frankly, I'm surprised that it's taken this long for this whole story to leak out.

And I would have expected nothing less because company loyalty doesn't matter much out West and job longevity is pretty much a joke. We may have fewer superstars in Chicago right now (that's changing as we speak), but, while the culture and the people here are just as competitive, we also value commitment and keeping your promises. Our best employees basically stick around. They're here and in it for the long haul – not for the easy exits – and not for the next best offer.

But that doesn't mean that there isn't a big issue around compensation in Chicago and every other tech-oriented big city these days that's causing a lot of headaches and heartaches for young entrepreneurs who are trying to build their businesses with limited capital.

I understand that in every market there's an ongoing competition for talent, but there's also a lot of talented engineers and others walking around these days wondering exactly what to do with themselves. There are a lot fewer sure things than you'd imagine; not everyone's got a game-changing idea or a world-beating business; and there's not all that much appeal (or upside) to becoming employee 98,001 at Apple.

And whether you want to acknowledge it or not, it's not a free or perfect market for talent anywhere because a great many of us are constrained by other considerations – family demands, education requirements, location and the risks of picking up and moving across the country, etc. – and these concerns also all factor into the choices that we can make.

So I think that right now it's almost as hard (however talented you may be) to find a great opportunity (and the one that's right for you) as it is for businesses to find all the talent they need. And I'd suggest that this is a healthy kind of equilibrium that serves us all in the long run and that should encourage all of us to try to keep our personnel costs somewhat in check.

As I imagine Jesse James used to say: it's always a better idea to rob the train first and then split up the loot. Or as Kanye says: **"I got a problem with spending before I get it. We all self-conscious. I'm just the first to admit it."**

OPTIMIZING, NOT MAXIMIZING, YOUR TEAM'S OUTPUT MATTERS MOST

Today, and every day from now on, the tools and technologies that permit us (and others) to observe and document more and more detailed information about everything that we (as well as all those around us) do, see, pay and say are continuing to exponentially increase their power, scope and accuracy. Data is the oil of the digital age and we are generating unfathomable amounts. Not only are we swimming in it; we're leaving a trail of digital exhaust everywhere we go to be captured, analyzed and output in real time and in ways that will increasingly permit third parties to anticipate and attempt to influence and change our behaviors. This flood of facts creates amazingly attractive opportunities and chilling challenges at the same time.

I'm not really concerned about big data and big government and the NSA; my interests are much closer to home and all about how we are using all this new information to most effectively manage and grow our businesses. I've said (practically forever) that keeping score matters and that, in most businesses, what gets measured (acknowledged and rewarded) is what gets done. I haven't changed my belief in this regard so much as I have come to believe that we are putting too much emphasis strictly on the numbers. Numbers don't lie, but they never tell the whole story. They can only take you so far before they top out and you need something more qualitative and experiential to get to the right conclusions.

Peter Drucker's dictum that: "if you can't measure it, you can't manage it" has created a whole generation of analysts and others who are often so focused on perfecting their business's processes that they lose sight of the business's purposes. I hear managers all the time talking about the need to get more work out of their people when they should be trying to get the best work out of them. Optimizing, not maximizing, the team's output is what matters most to the ultimate success of the business. Working smarter and more impactfully - not necessarily longer or harder - is how you ultimately move your business away from and ahead of the competition.

So I think that we have to be exceedingly careful these days that we don't let the ease of access and use and the ubiquity of massive amounts of quantitative performance data cause us to over-emphasize the math and measurements in our businesses (and in our lives) and thereby lose sight of the far more important qualitative attributes of what's going on and the meaning and value (rather than just the metrics) of our various activities. Not everything is easy to measure or quantify, but that doesn't make these things less important; it just makes our job as managers tougher. Human nature (being what it is) means we tend to gravitate toward the easy and the concrete rather than the harder and often vaguer vectors involving attitudes and behaviors. But when you get so comfortable with and wrapped up in the measurement process that it becomes a goal and an end in itself, you discover pretty quickly that it loses its effectiveness. In today's frenzied work world, it's easy to confuse movement with progress – but not all motion is forward – and lots of activities that run up the numbers aren't remotely productive. Measuring more is easy; measuring better is tough.

And when you let the numbers basically drive the train, you also give up two important advantages that are critical to your success. First, the goal isn't to be the thermometer; it's to be the thermostat. It's not about measuring the heat; it's about generating and controlling the heat. You don't want the analytics to lead you; they're a useful benchmark and a guide for course corrections, but it's on you to set the direction and move the business forward. Second, when you get so focused on specific and concrete financial results (sales targets, growth rates, etc.) and you direct all your team's energies toward getting as close to achieving those numbers as possible; you actually limit your ultimate upside because you lose the ability to think and see beyond those immediate goals. This means that when a game-changing opportunity, a quantum shift in your sales prospects, or an out-of-the-box new direction appears; your team may be so heads-down and in the weeds pushing those budget numbers that someone else will come along and grab the new brass ring.

I think that there's some middle ground here and some ideas that can help you balance the temptation to take the easy way out with the need to deal with all the facts – even the fuzzy ones – in order to get the full picture. Here are three important perspectives to keep in mind:

(1) Elaboration is a Form of Pollution

Tell your team to keep it simple. No one gets paid by the page or the pound and shorter is almost always better. I've found that when people expand and extend their plans, proposals and presentations, there's a high degree of likelihood that they're concerned about the value of their pitch so they try to bury it in a boatload of facts and figures, charts and citations, and everything else that just hides the hard truth. It's better for everyone for your people to put things right out there – front and center – and take their medicine if that's what's called for. If you torture the numbers long enough, they'll say whatever you like, but that's not any way to get to the truth or the right result.

(2) Not Everything is Worth Doing Well

Tell your team that everyone's always on the clock. There's an opportunity cost associated with everything we do and choosing what not to do and how extensively to do the things you need to do are critical in any startup which has scarce resources and even less time. One size or one approach never fits all of the possible cases. Some things just don't warrant the full court press and it's important to make sure that everyone knows that that's O.K. with you. Other things shouldn't be done at all and you should never try to do things cheaply that just aren't worth doing. It's never easy to turn people down or say "No" to marginal choices, but it's part of the job and comes with the territory.

(3) No One's Ever Measured How Much the Heart Can Hold

Ultimately, the value of the critical connections your people make every day with your clients and customers can only be roughly approximated by even the best math. But it's those daily personal and emotional interactions with your empowered employees that build the crucial engagement as well as the lifetime value of those buyers for your business. You need to give your team permission to do what's best for the customer in the moment that the opportunity arises. If they need to consult a rule book or have a calculator handy to do the math, they'll lose the value of the moment every time. The best businesses don't worry about the number or sheer volume of moments – they work to make each moment matter.

WHY RABBITS DON'T RUN BIG BUSINESSES

I've always been partial to Thumper's Dad's advice about communication. In case you don't recall it from the *Bambi* movie, his Dad said: "If you can't say something nice, don't say nothin' at all" - at least as Thumper recalled it. And, as it happens, this is pretty good advice for small talking animals, but it's a really bad way to run your company. You can't build a successful business based on a culture that values quiet, courtesy and consensus over honest conversations, constructive criticism and confrontations where necessary. Politely keeping the peace can't ever trump telling the truth. The best operators know two things for certain: (1) the truth only hurts when you don't tell it and (2) the truth only hurts when it should. I realize that sometimes it's very hard to tell the truth, but it's just as hard to hide it and a whole lot less productive.

White lies and other pleasantries are worthless – they're a lot like eating junk food – you get a temporary lift, but no nourishment; the problem persists; the emptiness returns; and nothing gets done in the meantime. And when you encourage people to lie even a little, you learn quickly that people who will lie for you will eventually lie to you. Better a few bruises and battered egos than a bankrupt business based on bullshitting each other. And honestly, it's just so much easier for everyone because when you always tell the truth, you never have to waste time and energy trying to remember your lies.

Frankly, an aggressive culture where people stand their ground and argue their cases makes for much better ultimate decisions as long as people are arguing for the right reasons. The right reasons are to get to the truth and the best results for the business and not because people need to be right and won't shut up until they grind everyone down and wear everyone else out. Make your point; say your piece; and sit your butt down. Don't argue with the truth.

You want your people to fearlessly face the facts. As one of the great old Hollywood moguls used to say: "I want my people to tell me the truth even if it costs them their jobs". But seriously, unpleasant facts don't fade away when you ignore them – they fester – and refusing to look at them won't change the situation or improve things until you do something about them. Facts may change, but the truth never does. And waiting only makes things worse. It's a funny thing about the truth – the truth doesn't have a time of its own. There's never a better or best time to tell someone the truth – the time for truth is always <u>now</u>.

I think all of the foregoing comes down to a few simple "rules" which you need to share (somewhat obsessively) with all of your people (not just newbies in orientations) on a regular and recurring basis. My suggested and very basic rules are as follows:

(1) <u>Tell the Truth</u>

No shades, no strokes, no "smoothing" the news or softening the blows – give it to me simple and straight. Figures don't lie, but they often don't tell the whole story. Make sure that the metrics don't get in the way of a clear message. As they say, everyone is entitled to their own opinion, but the facts are the facts – you don't get to pick and choose them.

(2) Tell It Timely

Nothing ugly really improves over time. Don't wait to bring me bad news. The sooner and shorter the better. I need a brief, not as book. Nothing elaborate – just accurate information delivered on time and in time.

(3) Tell Everyone

Don't assume that everyone else (or anyone else) necessarily knows what you know. Spread the word. In addition to the general virtues of transparency and making sure that eventually the message does get thru to the right people; going wide makes it more likely that meaningful and actionable information will also get to people who need whether you even realize that or not.

(4) Tell It 'til Someone Listens

I don't think that, in most businesses, you can <u>ever</u> over-communicate relevant and time-sensitive data. But you will often encounter people who fall into two problem piles: (a) people who don't want to say what nobody wants to hear; and (b) people who don't want to hear what needs to and has to be said and spread throughout the organization. These folks are master manipulators and they typically follow the standard three-step routine in dealing with "inconvenient", but sadly true facts: (i) first they aggressively ridicule; (ii) then they violently resist; and finally (iii) they get with the program – claim that they knew it all along – and treat things as obvious and self-evident. You need to keep spreading the word until you're sure that you've done as much as you can reasonably do to let the folks in charge know what you know. If they don't listen after that, so be it. It's frustrating and depressing, but in many businesses, it's a fact of life. As Bruce Springsteen says: "When the truth is spoken and it makes no difference – something in your heart goes cold". After a while, if it's clear that you're wasting your breath, find a better place to be.

(5) Tell It All the Time

And finally, truth-telling is not a sometime thing. As with everything else that matters in your business, it's an everyday, all day part of creating and maintaining an environment where the organization learns and grows and where things continue to improve through a constant iterative process. You can't make innovation through iteration work if you don't have a constant and accurate flow of data telling you what's working and what's not and where you're going wrong.

DON'T HIRE THE WRONG PERSON EVEN FOR A GOOD REASON

It's the holiday season and everyone wants to lend someone else a helping hand. But let me just say, without seeming too Grinch-like, that, while I heartily agree with the idea and the sentiment, it's important to remember that – even in the working world – charity begins at home. It's sweet to be Santa, but not if your business suffers as a result.

There's an old (and somewhat naïve) adage about friends and finance. When you're considering making a loan to a friend, you should give a lot of thought to which you'd most prefer not to lose: the money or the friend. The reason that the adage is naïve is that, in the vast majority of cases, you can almost certainly count on damaging the friendship and/or losing the friend entirely – even if you get the money paid back.

There's something about being in debt to a friend that's awkward and humbling and just never bodes well for the long-term life of the relationship. So it's much smarter (albeit not often easy) to be a good enough friend to give your buddy a straight and simple "no" rather than starting down the slippery slope of becoming a lender. Better a friendly refusal than an unwilling promise.

I got to thinking about this when one of our startup CEOs asked me an interesting question recently about hiring. He had heard me talking about the "Hotel California" syndrome here at 1871 – that's the idea that no one ever really leaves our place even if their particular business idea doesn't work out. As The Eagles' song says: "you can check out any time you like, but you can never leave".   Instead, at 1871, the smartest of the guys whose businesses have gone sideways or who've run out of cash before they found their footing or their market niche have an interesting reaction.

They don't sulk. They don't make excuses. They don't expect the world to owe them a living. Instead, they get busy. They start looking around; they do their research and homework, and then they try to attach themselves to a better and hopefully more viable idea at another member company with more traction and momentum. It's very Darwinian, it's productive, and it works all day long.

I think that this is one of 1871's greatest accomplishments – to have built an organic community that's so additive and supportive of everyone here that it's almost as if there's a safety net that assures a soft landing and a new start for the serious and committed folks who want to stay in the game, get right back up in the saddle, and get rolling again.

Now, of course, there are two sides to this process and honestly the job's a lot harder for those on the helping and hiring side than it is for the guys (and girls) looking for their next gig. And that difficulty, in fact, was exactly the subject matter of the question which I was asked.

It went something like this: How do I figure out if it makes sense for me (and for my company) to hire someone whose business just blew up? Especially if it's someone I feel like I know pretty well; who I think is smart and committed; and someone who's been working 3 desks away from me for the last year – head down – 24/7 – balls to the wall? In fact, I have to admit, that there were plenty of weeks when – just watching from the sidelines - I felt like a slacker compared to this guy. So really, what more about him (or her) do I need to know and what are the right questions that I need to ask in order to find out whether this is a smart hire?

I'd say that there are five basic questions that you need to ask the person and to get clear and convincing answers to before you move forward. And, by the way, don't expect this to be an easy or comfortable conversation. It should be hard and it should be honest because it's important to get this right at the outset or you'll regret it for a long time later.

So here are my five questions:

(1) Are You Done with Your Dream?

It's not ever easy for an entrepreneur to give up on his dream, but it's essential for you to make sure that you're not paying someone to work for you whose head really isn't into the game and who's spending the bulk of his time and emotion trying to figure out how to resuscitate his old business and get the show back on the road. There's no lie detector test for this kind of thing – you've just got to look each other in the eye and decide whether there's a real commitment to leave the past behind so that you can count on getting the full attention and energy that are required directed toward the success of your business

(2) Are You Down with My Dream?

It's easy to fall in love when you need a job. That's not enough of a commitment to make things work in the start-up world because it's never just a job. It's signing up to give the dream everything you've got and you really have to care about the vision, about making a difference (not just a paycheck), and your heart needs to be in the game just as fully as your head. This is an essential part of the down-and-dirty conversation that needs to take place and the best candidates will tell you upfront what they like about your idea and your program and what they think could be changed or could be better. But they can't be signing on with the idea that - once they're in the clubhouse - they'll have a chance to start rearranging the furniture and changing things. They need to buy into your dream and then help make it better – not try to turn it into their dream. And they need to sign on 100% on Day One. If they have serious reservations, they need to work someplace else.

(3) Are You Already Ready to Re-Up?

A dying dream is a debilitating thing and sometimes we don't even realize at the outset just how hard a hit we took or the extent of the damage done. It takes a while for the reality to sink in and for all the conversations to take place where a hundred random people ask you how your business is doing and you have to break the news to them. Every one of those "chats" is just more salt in the wound that you were hoping was getting better every day. I get that it's great to get over the past and pick yourself up off the floor and move forward, but you also need to catch your breath and make sure you're settled before you start off on the next adventure. Catching someone too soon on the rebound isn't any better an idea in your business affairs than it is in your love life. Make sure the new guy is really ready to start and knows what he's signing up for.

(4) Are You Sure You Can Be Second Chair?

There's only one seat at the top and one captain of the ship and you need to make sure that everyone understands the pecking order from the get-go. And, just to be clear, this isn't just something to get straight between you and the new hire – it's important that it's clear to the whole team so that everyone knows what to expect and how to proceed. It's easy to fall into a trap here and start talking (while you're still in the "selling" mode of convincing the guy to come on board) about being "partners" in the journey and working closely together. And, while that's a good ultimate goal, it's a bad way to start the new relationship off. You're the boss in your business. He or she used to be the boss in their prior businesses. The new relationship needs to be clearly understood from Day One.

(5) Are You in It for the Long Run?

You don't want to waste your time and money training and integrating the new guy into your business if he simply regards it as a stop-over on his way to his next start-up. You're not a way station to anywhere and – while there are no guarantees that anything will last forever or that everyone will ever work out perfectly, you can't afford to have someone coming into the business who already has one foot out the door. Make sure they're there for the duration or don't do the deal.

I feel a little like Smokey the Bear talking about an ounce of prevention and going through these things which should be fairly obvious to all of us, but which, in fact, too often get lost or overlooked when we're in a hurry to get a good new guy on the team. All I can say is that it's a lot better to avoid the potholes entirely than it is to get a great deal on the towing service that comes to bail you out of the hole.

THE CURSE OF COHORTS

If you thought it was difficult to start a new business in the education space, you'd be right for sure. But it's even harder to do something in the adult education space and that's very unfortunate because we - as a country - are in dire need of more companies providing cost-effective and results-oriented retraining and up-skilling programs especially to adult learners whether they be career changers, new job seekers, or just folks whose continued employment and value to their companies is in question because their own skills haven't kept up with the growing technical and digital requirements of their jobs.

Having large numbers of people in any of these three particular populations sitting on the sidelines looking for new opportunities without having the requisite training for the new positions which are available and currently going unfilled represents major losses to our economy - not merely because these individuals aren't working - but also because they represent a wealth of accumulated institutional knowledge that will be lost if we can't figure out how to connect and enable them with the new technologies and move them and their aggregated wisdom forward and into the digital economy. So creating better and more effective systems of adult education and re-skilling are critical, but they're hard and especially hard for startups mainly for one overwhelming reason.

I call it the "curse of cohorts" and it's a bitch. School teachers and even college professors by and large have it easy in the cohort department. As I used to tell my faculty, sadly we keep getting older while the students every year are the same age and, of course, that's precisely the point. Our traditional education system does the selection, segmentation and other sorting for us so basically the majority of students in any class are roughly the same in terms of demographics, prior experience and education, and - maybe most importantly - expectations and aspirations. Classes are for all intents and purposes cohorts by definition and can be addressed and dealt with from a curricular perspective in a single and consistent fashion.

I don't mean that their individual needs are the same or that they will be learning in the same way or that they should even be taught in the same manner because differentiated learning is the future of all education. And don't get me started on how stupid the "one size fits all" model of teaching is. But at least in a given group within a given class, there will be some prerequisites and some fundamental external and known alignments. And we also know for sure that their common and overriding objective is to complete the class and graduate.

Unfortunately when you get to adult education, it's a vastly different ballgame. It's almost impossible to figure out who will respond to your ads (in whatever channels you launch them) and realistically what each and every one of the prospects will be expecting to get in the class and to get out of the class. I used to joke that, if you announced a class on Excel, you'd have respondents looking for a new headache cure; rank beginners who'd never used a spreadsheet; and masters looking for new strategies to crank up their pivot tables, etc. A course on Ruby on Rails would unearth model railroaders and aspiring gemologists among others searching for the keys to the kingdom.

And those are just the types of disconnects that arise regularly over subject matter and course materials and coverage. When you add to that unwieldy mess, the additional and considerable confusion over outcomes, next steps, and what the extent of the actual preparation is expected to be, it's amazing that anyone can manage this process at all. Some of the students expect that 12 weeks of coding instruction will turn them into entrepreneurs; others plan to immediately jump into a mid-level, high-paying programming job at a major corporation, and still others think that - with enough passion and energy - you can actually wish a real business into existence. Turning even the best ideas into invoices takes a lot more than that. In fact, the matchmaking function itself may be the absolutely hardest part of building a sustainable and profitable adult education business.

Frankly, if I had the time, I'd quickly build a national registry of the course offerings from all the different providers in every city that would be the "go-to", one-stop place to find exactly what you were looking for. It would have its own tipping-point mechanism built right in so that each specific class would launch and go forward only after the minimum required number of appropriate and interested people had actually signed up for it. Hard to believe that it doesn't already exist, and yet, it doesn't. But, alas, that's for another day.

Right now, if you're intent on trying to help in this space, I've got plenty of scars, lots of experience, and some specific tips for you.

(1) Find A Channel (Outbound)

Trying to reach your cohort of ready, willing and able students (who are also qualified) among an unbelievably diverse population of potential adult learners who are hopefully interested in precisely your particular offering in a specific location and at fixed times and dates is an expensive and ridiculously expensive proposition and one which (if you were to tell the truth) has continual customer acquisition costs far in excess of what you can realistically charge a given student for your course offering. You're not gonna make it up in the volume either. Because unlike a college or university, too many adult courses are one-off deals where there isn't even a way to claim that you can amortize your acquisition costs over multiple sessions or courses which will eventually be taken by each person once you've incurred the cost to track them down and attract them to your program. This is much harder than finding a needle in a haystack – it's more like continually sticking yourself with the needle and hoping that eventually you'll get used to the pain.

So you need an outbound, cost-effective communication channel to reach your targets. You want to ride on someone else's back and rely on their bucks to help you get the job done. This is a lot easier than you think because fashioning win-win partnerships these days are all the rage. In particular, membership organizations a (think AAA or AARP) are all under growing pressure to demonstrate the value they provide to their members in order to retain them when so many of the things they traditionally offered to their groups are now available elsewhere and often at no cost. So find yourself a free ride – associations, membership organizations, alumni groups, etc. and choose the ones most closely aligned to your offerings and see what happens.

(2) Find A Feeder (Inbound)

A staggering number of traditional schools (high schools, colleges and universities) aren't giving their graduates the concrete and practical skills that these students need to secure one of the massive number of good-paying and challenging jobs which are being created in the digital economy every day. We need more vocational training at every level of the education chain and this is the precise niche that high-end, technical adult education programs can fill if we regard them as "finishing" schools and education extenders and enhancers rather than as places for grown-ups to occasionally pursue their hobbies, dreams and passions.

The traditional schools aren't going to get around to changing their programs any time soon (the community colleges are actually beating them to the punch), but their students (and graduates) are starting to get the picture and they make great targets for these kinds of programs even before they're officially done with school. It's easier than you would imagine to get the word out about what you're doing on college campuses and much, much less expensive than other channels. Keep in mind that the students still do listen to certain of their professors and they have considerable sway. You never know how valuable a testimonial or an endorsement can be in helping to convince your prospects to sign up with you until you run into a situation where you're the one without someone else in your corner helping to vouch for and "sell" your product or service. Having two Profs pitching your programs is worth a lot more than piles of pamphlets at the student union or persistent emails and other promotions.

(3) Find A Food Chain (Upward Bound)

More and more, the singly most discouraging words that I hear from the "graduates" of so many of these short-term courses is that – now that they have made the investment, spent the time, and learned whatever, they really don't know where to go or what to do next – either because the actual training they've received is only part of the story (some, but not all, of the skills or tools that they need to really move forward in their job search, etc.) or because there's no placement support or service from the training provider to help them take the next critical steps.

Now I realize that - as good as your intentions may be - you can't do everything for people and you can't push or pull people forward all by yourself. All you can do is to show them a possible future and a defined path to get there. You can tell them everything that is necessary and just what it takes to succeed, but you can't understand these things for them. Ultimately, it's on them. But it's up to you to show them that there is a path for them and that it's real and manageable if they're willing to make the effort. It's simply not enough for you to mentally draw some invisible line and take the position that your responsibility stops there.

I realize that it's one whole and pretty difficult task to just do a great job at the education part of the process and that most of the people offering these courses aren't even equipped (and they certainly don't have the necessary time and/or resources) to run a placement service when – very frankly – they're constantly scrapping to fill their own next bunch of classes. So – if you can't do it yourself, it's critically important to make yourself a place in one or more food chains and become a feeder to the groups and organizations who need the very people that you're training – even if the training isn't one hundred percent of their requirements – because they're not only the logical employers, they're also willing and able and equipped to fill in the missing gaps with their own on-boarding processes. It's another win-win situation. You inexpensively source qualified and interested people for them – they fill the bill and finish the process further down the line for you.

IT'S IMPORTANT TO EAT
YOUR OWN DOGFOOD

While VCs often talk in their peculiar shorthand about quickly figuring out whether a certain startup's customers – regardless of their species or breed – are going to eat the company's dog food (meaning a newly-introduced product or service); it's equally important for the company's management to make sure – whenever it's appropriate – that their own team members are also fully committed to the business's own offerings and that they're using them as much and as often as possible. The car guys in Detroit figured this out (sadly it was one of the few things they did) when it was made clear to every employee that it was absolutely verboten to even think of driving a foreign car to your job at Ford or GM.

This wasn't ever simply a loyalty test – it's just a fact of life that it's much easier and more convincing for someone in sales to provide his or her own testimonial and to demonstrate through examples from their own actual experience the value and benefits of what they're selling. You never want to be the shoemaker's kids and you never want to be in the position of urging someone else to do something that you haven't or wouldn't do yourself. It's just not credible. No one should ever take advice from someone who doesn't have to live with the consequences.

At 1871, we use the tools, apps and products of a number of our member companies who started out here because (a) we should and (b) because they work. Then we make it our business to spread the word. And that's why I'm so impressed with the Chicago-based branch of the Startup Institute which is located within 1871 and which is just cranking out amazing results – not only in their own operations – but, more importantly, in terms of providing a constant and growing stream of talented and excited new employees for so many of our member companies.

I think that 1871 companies alone are hiring about 10% to 15% of each Startup Institute cohort as they graduate from the program. Some of these firms have already hired 4 or 5 people from the SI program and they keep coming back for more. In terms of attracting, training and retaining talent for Chicago companies in general, over 90 Chicago-based businesses as well as major corporations have employed SI graduates and alumni so far. This is pretty big news for an operation that's only been at it for a relatively short time.

As it happens, the overall population of 1871 aligns almost ideally with the target populations which the Startup Institute seeks to train. This is why I think it's working so well for all concerned. We have newbies for sure. We have career changers. We have smart folks with real experience who need a tech and digital refresh – or better yet – a couple of partners. We have people that did one thing for a long, long time and are now looking to pursue their passion. And we have plenty of folks full of energy and passion who are looking for the right place to make a difference.

But what's most interesting about the whole situation is what it says about the kinds of employees that both our early-stage businesses as well as the companies entering the growth stage are going to need to keep adding to their teams. And, if you're running a startup anywhere, there's a lesson here for you as well.

One surprising hint: it's not just about programmers, engineers and other techies. And it's also not just newbies or people looking for their first jobs right out of school. Our businesses need (1) talented sales people, (2) serious management help as they scale, (3) domain experts to help identify real customer needs and requirements, and (4) even a little gray hair.

And that's where the unique make-up of the day-to-day population of 1871 comes in. Very few people realize just how diverse and robust a group of entrepreneurs can be when you have 1500 people a day showing up at your doorstep. Each day. Every day. One particularly interesting fact is that our largest single group of members is composed of people with more than 14 years of industry experience. Not youngsters and not newbies.

1871 today isn't just about any one group or type of individuals. It's not just for people interested in tech – in no small part - because tech is a part of everything today. You couldn't avoid being tech-enabled if you tried. Nor is 1871 limited or appropriate only just for people of a certain age or only for those interested in simply a single industry or market sector. Passion, innovation, inspiration and entrepreneurship come in every size and shape and we welcome them all.

And the most important thing that you learn about people when you're building a business – which is the very reason that the alumni of the Startup Institute make such great hires and can hit the ground running and start making a difference immediately – is that to build a great business, you need all kinds of people with different attitudes, aptitudes and abilities. Trying to hire only people who look, act and reason just like you is a fool's mission. It's the diversity of ideas and even ideals that makes all the difference.

YOUR KEY EMPLOYEES AREN'T FUNGIBLE - THEY'RE INVALUABLE

You would think it would be clear that any business's most valuable workers aren't multi-colored (but otherwise uniform) Checkers pieces (although – given their varying skills and capabilities - they might be more properly thought of as chessmen) which can be swayed, swapped, moved around and motivated at will. But this fact of life is apparently not obvious to millions of managers at every level in organizations of all sizes who continue to believe that – in almost everything involving people – one size or one approach fits all.

As we try to bring innovative and entrepreneurial behaviors into all kinds of industries, we find that - especially the senior managers - functionally assume (even though we obviously know better in our hearts) that – in a world of radical and constant changes – within and outside of our own businesses - every one of our team members will accept and react to the new and challenging behaviors that these changes will require gladly, readily and in the same fashion. This approach seems to be largely because we remain stuck with the last remnants of the tired old thinking that was derived from the precepts of the industrial revolution and thereafter deployed in both our schools and in many of our businesses.

In the schools, we're still trying to teach everyone the same things at the same time. Too many schools believe that one size fits all and that a single solution and a single "sage on the stage" spewing wisdom to a room full of sleepy students is the way to go and further that everyone there will actually learn the same things at the same rate. This is the last gasp of the mechanical factory model and it's hard to kill because – truth be told – it's cheap, it's orderly, and it's a lot less work for the teachers as well.

But don't blame most of the teachers – they'd much rather be actually teaching than spending a big part of every day with bureaucratic bullshit and paperwork. This whole educational system is beyond stupid, but it's so very, very slow to change. Differentiated learning ("to each his or her own") is the only approach that makes the slightest sense and we have the inexpensive tools, tablets and other technologies that can make it a reality today if we only have the will to make it so. (See my prior INC. education posts: http://www.inc.com/howard-tullman/why-education-needs-innovation.html and http://www.inc.com/howard-tullman/chicago-teachers-and-entrepreneurs.html. Here's hoping that the schools start to improve sometime soon.

We have a different variation of the same problem in too many businesses today. We think that everyone has basically learned the identical things in school and therefore that they will – by and large – perform in the same manner with roughly the same results and outcomes. We're still judging these employee "books" by their covers (and evaluating recent graduates by their inflated grades and grandiose degrees) instead of taking the time to test and determine the real skill sets and benefits that each of them brings to our businesses and, more importantly, the real impact that each of them can have on our company's workflow, overall efficiency, other employees, and bottom line. Credentials and degrees are a long way from competencies – they're basically crutches for lazy HR people – just as org charts and job descriptions don't begin to tell you what's really going on in your company.

People (and today's typical management tools) haven't changed in a long, long time and the rules are still the same: what gets measured is what supposedly gets done. Most people do what you inspect and not (sadly) what you expect. But, even though every day our analytical capacities grow and we have more and more data available about almost every aspect of our employees' performance, it turns out that very often we aren't paying attention to the right and most important metrics. We pay way more attention to punctuality than to productivity. We've got plenty of measurements, but they don't tell us the real story. And we're drowning in data that doesn't help us determine who's really driving the bus.

In order to make a material difference as managers and change agents, and to effectively bring about the important improvements and advances needed in our organizations, we have to be quantifying and measuring our key people's individual impact and influence, rather than merely gathering stats and information about their attendance or their relative positions. Only when we have a new and clear perspective on which of our employees can – directly and indirectly – be the most helpful in promulgating the attitudes and behaviors required for the desired changes can we figure out which of them can help us get the critical messages across to the remainder of the team. And given that better than 75% of all new initiatives introduced in large organizations fail; it's beyond critical to find these people in your own organization sooner rather than later if you want to be responsive to the ever-changing demands of the marketplace and stay competitive.

The good news is that, as you might expect, there are new data and analytics-based startups which are creating the tools that the biggest and smartest companies and other institutions will use to more effectively determine how to deploy and position their best employees and how to optimize the performance and impact of those key players. One of the most interesting new companies I have seen in a while is Syndio (https://synd.io) which creates actionable analytics about people in organizations of all sizes. But in doing so, the Syndio folks start from a slightly different place than you might expect.

It's a simple twist, but it makes a big difference. We all understand that, in rolling out just about anything, it pays to get the "good guys" on your side including the leaders, the stars, the celebs, and even the loud (and often obnoxious) voices that people will often listen to for whatever reason. We think of these people as "influencers" and we all get that it's better to have them in our camp rather than resisting our programs or dumping on our ideas.

But it often turns out – especially as companies grow – that we only think we know who these people are and we're often wrong. Lots of these folks are "all hat and no cattle" as my friends in Texas like to say and sometimes the most effective folks are actually the "friends in low places" rather than the blowhards in the big offices. A couple of critical care nurses in a hospital can save more lives by modeling and enforcing good hand-washing disciplines (among the staff and the doctors) than most of the surgeons I the course of a year.

And even if and when we can identify and pick the right types of people; what the science of networks and influence says about delivering really effective campaigns and results is somewhat different than you'd guess. It turns out that, although the people are undoubtedly important – role models, change agents, information spreaders - among others, the real gating factor is their relative positions within and the strength and size of their networks within the business. It just so happens that a movement can be started or a systemic change effectively initiated and grown within an organization just as easily by a mere mortal with a strong set of internal connections (and a powerful message) as it is can be by some superstar orator, politician or other impassioned advocate. Whole governments in the Arab Spring were brought low by the selfless and desperate acts of a few individuals.

But the trick is that - without new tools and systems – growing businesses and large organizations are highly unlikely to find all of these people and properly recruit them to the cause. As a result, their new initiatives and programs are diluted and far less impactful than they could and should be. They need programs like Syndio's which overlay their traditional HR data with the new social and network analytics that identify and quantify the real, respected movers and shakers and the scale and scope of their influence networks within the business.

Syndio can implement these types of analytics quickly and easily for virtually everyone in a given workforce without any significant hit to ongoing operations or existing information or HR systems. And, once they are in place, they actually become bi-directional tools as well. Not only can the management's messages be more effectively distributed; these identified individuals can and do regularly become the sources for all manner of input and feedback from the field which would not otherwise be available at all to the senior management team. It's a benefit with a double bottom line.

But the real bottom line is very simple. Top down communications in business today are largely a waste of time and breath. Treating your employees as a homogeneous population to which you can broadcast a single message won't work any better for your business than it has for the TV networks of old. Peer to peer, customized communications to and from people we are directly and regularly connected with and whose opinions we value and respect are the only ways we want to learn today. People don't commit much of anything to companies today – they commit to other people.

DEMOCRACY IN BUSINESS ISN'T THE BE-ALL AND END-ALL

We hear a lot of disparaging comments and complaints these days about the hyper-inclusive management style of many early-stage businesses and how it's hindering their progress and growth. I'm sure you've heard some of these statements as well and they're not all simply cases of unhappy whiners or sour grapes. In many cases, it's a serious issue and, as the workforce continues to get younger, it's going to become a bigger problem. It's fixable in most cases, but only if it's addressed, explained, clarified and resolved in a straightforward and honest manner. People like to know who's actually leading the charge in their company, what their roles are, what's expected (and not expected from them) and where the business is headed. But, in some young and fast-growing companies, because so much of the organization is in flux and constantly in transition, it's hard to determine who's actually running things and who can make a binding decision that will stick. If the finality of decisions turns on who was the loudest and who was the last to get in the face of the CEO, the place is doomed.

A lot of this carping may just be background noise, but I think that there's also some substance to these discussions that's definitely worth thinking about for a bit. You hear wisecracks about founders letting "the inmates" run the asylum in the name of equality or democracy and that, as a result, those businesses are headed right into the ground.

Or you read angry rants about the need to "get the amateurs off the field" so that the real professionals can take over. I don't really think that this is just an age thing or purely the province of people who are fundamentally resistant to change. It's more philosophical than that and it has much more to do with figuring out a good governance strategy for your company than it does with gray hair.

And, as easy as it would be to write these conversations off as just the latest manifestation of the generational conflicts that are seemingly rampant in so many businesses today, it's a much harder argument to make when you're talking about startups where there really aren't as many age gaps as you might find in larger and more established businesses. Just because most of the people in your business are roughly the same age doesn't automatically mean that they're in accord about how and who should run the show and who should be included in what decisions.

It's less an age thing and more a culture thing which depends largely on where they've been and where they're coming from and actually how they were raised. There are plenty of people these days who buy into ideas like radical transparency and complete information sharing or participatory management at all levels because they heard it in school or from others without having seen how wrong some of these experiments have gone or having tried to manage systems like this. You can be totally sincere and very passionate about your feelings, but still be completely wrong about what's good for the business. And the sooner you get straightened out, the happier and more productive you'll be. Or, if it's not for you, you'll be gone. Organizations can grow through adoption or attrition – either way works. You can get with the program or you can go elsewhere.

And frankly, it's not really your call anyway. Good businesses aren't run by majority rule. You may all be in the same bed, but everyone's got their own dreams and their own obligations and responsibilities.

Collaboration and community and Kumbuya are all cool things, but – in a crunch or a crisis – it's the CEO's job to make the hard calls and everyone else's job to line up behind the decision and execute the plan. Period. Full stop.

At a certain point, even for the CEO, seeking more input from more people is as much about putting off the tough calls as it is about further informing yourself or arming yourself with more ammunition. Expanding the decision set and waiting to decide almost never results in a better outcome. Better the best decision you can make at the time based on the data you have available than delaying the decision until it becomes a crisis where your choices and options are fewer and less attractive.

And, as it turns out, the data acquisition and evaluation issues are actually the less challenging parts of the problem. The bigger and more difficult issue has to do with managing the expectations and the emotions of your people. This is where the wickets can quickly get sticky and where no good deed ever goes unpunished. You can repeatedly explain things to people, but you can't understand for them. It's very hard to tell someone that their participation isn't required (or that their input isn't being solicited) without essentially telling them that their opinions don't matter and yet that's basically the exact truth – at least as to some areas of the business. This is especially difficult today because (particularly in a new business) everyone considers themselves an expert on almost everything.

Bottom line – it's always going to be hard to tell people what they don't want to hear and it's never going to get easier, but it's essential to the integrity and effectiveness of your decision-making and your company's operation. And while no two situations or businesses are exactly alike, I think there are a few critical considerations that you – as the boss and the one ultimately accountable for the final decisions and the consequences - need to take into account.

1. Democracy in decision-making is diverting and delusional.

If everything that's up for discussion is also up for grabs because it's subject to further changes, second-guessing, and unending debate and everyone in the place is entitled to not merely an opinion, but a vote on everything; nothing worthwhile will ever get done. This creates major roadblocks (both inside and outside the business) to getting the right things done in a timely fashion. As I wrote in an earlier INC. piece, it's pretty clear to anyone with any real management experience that not everything in any business is everyone's business. See http://www.inc.com/howard-tullman/with-this-much-help-youll-never-get-anything-done.html. Not everyone's opinion is necessary or valuable; not everyone's ideas are great or need to be considered; not everyone knows what they're talking about; and – in any event – consistent unanimity is never essential to a strong and effective decision-making process. It's just another fantasy from the four guys who started in the garage. All for one and one for all is fine for a slogan, but having too many cooks in the kitchen makes for some very sorry soup.

2. Democracy in meetings is demoralizing and debilitating.

Meetings don't run themselves unless they're being run by morons. There needs to be a meeting leader and the leader needs to be a good listener, but even more than that, he or she needs to be a good chooser and a great editor. It's also not a popularity contest. It doesn't have to be a rude process, but it does have to be ruthless in protecting the purpose of the meeting, moving things along, cutting off people who are off track or off message, and managing the outcome of the discussion in the time allotted. Democracy in meetings is not a value in and of itself and trying to pretend otherwise is a waste of everyone's time and dysfunctional as well.

Business meetings are neither occupational therapy sessions nor venues for free expression. If they have a valuable purpose at all, it's about getting things discussed and decided and not about giving everyone in the room scrupulously equal air time to express themselves and to share whatever thoughts may have serendipitously popped into their heads. Just because something occurred to you doesn't necessarily make it interesting or valuable to me. In meetings, it's a lot better to make one person unhappy than to suck the life out of the entire group by making them suffer through someone's enthusiastic, but stupid, suggestions.

3. Democracy in design is dumb.

Style and design talents aren't things that are remotely equally distributed in the general population and certainly not among the employees in your company. There are people who are really good at these things and that's why you find and employ them. You need to commit to and trust a talented design team and express a simple vision and set of objectives to them and then get out of their way. This isn't a class project where everybody gets to try their hand. I've concluded that design committees are the singly most useless entities in the history of collaborative enterprise and - without exception - result in wasted time and money as well as a crappy outcome because they operate on two equally stupid principles: (a) the design which is least objectionable to the most people on the committee will be the best design; and (b) if each committee member gets something incorporated into the design which is near and dear to his or her heart, then everyone on the committee will be happy and that's all that really matters. The quality of the design is subordinated to the comfort and convenience of the committee.

4. Democracy in dollars is demotivating and destructive.

People aren't stupid and trying to paint them all with the same brush or compensate them all in roughly the same way is the easiest and quickest way to lose your best people and demotivate even the good ones who stay while they're looking for their next job. (See the very unhappy experiences of Dan Price, the founder of Gravity Payments, who tried to scale up the pay of everyone in his company to at least $70k a year for a very cautionary tale.) We used to call the folks who stuck around, but stopped caring "people who quit without leaving" and they are super-bad for your business. You've got to pay people what each of them is really worth to the business in terms of both their value and their contributions (as well as their judgment and experience) and you've got to make it clear to the rest of the team that this is exactly how the world should work. The people who contribute the most (not necessarily those who simply work the most) are the ones who will earn the most. And even more to the point – people with highly-specialized and valuable skills are often worth a multiple of what you might be paying other team members – especially in our highly-competitive talent market. If people don't think that's fair, they're free to go work elsewhere.

There's a reason that democracy rhymes with mediocrity. Compromise and consensus are at the core of democracy, but they have almost nothing to do with creativity or with supporting and promoting the kinds of singular visions and ideas that are most likely to change the world.

COMPANY CULTURE, NOT THE COMPETITION, MATTERS MOST IN RECRUITING AND RETAINING TECH TALENT

I moderated a HR panel last week with Shawn Riegsecker, the CEO-founder of Centro (http://www.inc.com/profile/centro) in Chicago, and two of his senior tech talent recruiters. Centro is an ad-tech firm which already has over 700 employees in some 37 offices spread across the country. They've been ranked as the city's Best Place to Work for 4 or 5 years running in the Crain's Chicago survey; they've almost doubled their headcount in the last 18 months; and they don't see any end in sight. Like everyone else, the team at Centro is trying to hire all of the top tech talent they can get their hands on in order to support their continuing growth and the expanding demand for their services. And, of course, they're competing for that A-level talent with 100-plus other Chicago-based technology companies which are growing just as fast or even faster. Great news for the city's tech scene – not so much for the recruiters on the hot seats to get the job done.

But even considering how much pressure they're constantly under to grow, and as crazy as the talent competition all around them is, their strategies and the ideas that came through in our discussion were extremely thoughtful and long-term. The four main concepts - which I think are relevant to any fast-moving and fast-growing business today - were: (a) their personnel energies are primarily focused inside their business – they believe that building and maintaining their company culture is the key to recruiting and retaining the best people – not worrying about the competition; (b) they're in a hurry, but not hurried – they have a lengthy, multi-person, and quite diverse interview process and they're sticking to it - especially because it sends the right messages to their current employees and to prospective hires as well; (c) they understand that the things that worked for them in the past and got them this far (like a hugely impactful internal cash bonus program for new employee referrals) aren't sufficient to keep them moving forward and ahead of the pack, so they're constantly looking for new tools and better ways to get the job done; and (d) they're struggling – right along with every other tech firm – with how they can make their workforce more diverse even though – in terms of gender – they're already as diverse as any firm in the city.

(1) You Didn't Find Me, I Found You

The only thing better and more rewarding than finding and recruiting a super-talented new employee is learning that the prospect in question actually sought out your company and found you. Forget that this is highly efficient and cost-effective, it tells you that your culture is spreading beyond your four walls and that you've succeeded in developing an authentic, word -of-mouth (not manufactured) reputation as the one of the right places to be. You can't make this stuff up – you've got to live it every day and model the behaviors that matter. But as you do and as the critical attitudes and actions spread from the CEO throughout the entire company, you'll quickly learn that nothing is more contagious than a shared vision and a set of sincere and compelling corporate values. In the best companies, people don't come for the job, they come to be part of the vision and to spend their time in a place that values and appreciates them doing work that makes a difference.

(2) If I'm Not Growing, I'm Going

A definite key to successful retention was the idea that all of the employees needed to feel cared about and listened to by the company's senior management and especially by the CEO. An important part of all great companies' cultures are the (sometimes apocryphal) stories passed down over the years of special efforts, extraordinary gestures, and honored commitments by the founders and senior management as well as instances where they put the welfare and concerns of the employees ahead of their own. Centro has plenty of those tales especially during the 2008 recession when the first people to take pay cuts were the senior executives. But, even more important, has been the ongoing need for each employee to feel and believe that the company was committed to their own continued education and growth. Centro pays 100% of its employees' tuition costs for educational courses each year. Bottom line: if your key employees don't see a commitment, a path and a future full of promise, they're unlikely to be sticking around.

(3) Doing Things the Same Way Doesn't Make for Better Results

Centro has a reputation for promoting from within and it's another important element of the overall company culture. But if you're looking only at your existing employees for new management, you're not likely to be introducing the numbers of change agents and alternative thinkers that you'll need to drive real innovation. Companies and systems get stale without new blood and people with different perspectives being added regularly to the mix. Similarly, Centro has an amazingly successful employee referral system which pays their team members a cash bonus for each new hire they refer. This in-house program has historically accounted for well over 50% of their new employees and it's working like a charm, but it's not sourcing a diverse enough population of leads because the vast majority of the folks the employees know tend to be like them and look like them and that hasn't helped the company identify the kind and number of qualified minority candidates that they need to broaden their overall workforce. So they're looking into other channels including outside recruiters. But the most important thing they are doing is focusing on rapidly advancing their qualified minority employees into higher levels of management so that there's increased visibility and concrete demonstrations of the company's commitment to this goal.

(4) I Can Make You Better, But I Can't Make You Care

Centro prioritizes skills and character in their hiring. You've got to have the right skills to make the cut, but you're not really welcome if you don't have the character and the values that the company was built on from the beginning. I don't care how much you know until I know how much you care. You can fix a bad fit by changing someone's position or responsibilities or upskill a motivated and committed worker so he or she can do a better job and that's the kind of commitment that a great business makes to its people; but there's no cure for a crappy character except the door as soon as possible. Keeping someone around who's destructive or corrosive (however productive or talented they may be) is a cancer for the company and it's never too soon to tell these folks to take a hike. Hire slow, fire fast.

TIMELY TIPS FROM BILL RANCIC

We had the opportunity recently to host Bill Rancic – the first winner on Donald Trump's The Apprentice television program – for a keynote speech about what he's learned from several important mentors (he didn't mention The Donald which wasn't really that much of a surprise); how he's started and built his several entrepreneurial ventures; and finally a very important lesson that he took away from his triumph on the TV show in 2004 which, as he noted, seems like light years ago.

I thought that his explanation for how he won the Apprentice competition was very enlightening. He didn't say he worked the hardest. He didn't say he wanted it the most. And he certainly didn't say he was the smartest guy in the room. What he said made all the difference was something that we talk about every day at 1871 as well. It's the idea that nobody does anything important and worthwhile today all by themselves. You need a team to make the dream come true.

Bill said the key to his success was that he tried to "be the conductor" just like the main man at the symphony and that he used his talents to bring everyone together so they could make beautiful music. He knew – just like in the case of the orchestra - that he didn't personally have the special skills or the same abilities that each of the other members of his team had, but he was able to get them all moving in the right direction and to bring out the best effort that each team member had to contribute.

And he also knew that the most amazing things get done when no one cares who gets the credit. Harmony trumps hubris – no pun intended. It certainly wasn't easy – he had some confrontations and some hard sledding, but he always kept in mind what Robert Schuller said: "tough times never last, but tough people do!" And he never spent his time blaming others when things went wrong. That would have been a waste of breath and energy.

After the show, when he started working in the real world, he said he was fortunate to have some great people to learn from and whose examples he follows to this day. And he was smart enough and modest enough to know that, until he really knew what he was doing, it was a mistake to try to do things on his own. He needed to play a role for a while before he tried to roll his own even though one of his first ventures was in the mail order cigar business. See http://www. inc.com/howard-tullman/entrepreneurship-will-you-sink-or-swim. html.

Bill had a very clear idea of where he wanted to end up and even how he thought he would get there, but he was smart enough to know that these things were going to take some time and that the smartest thing he could do in the meantime was to concentrate on learning something from someone every day on the journey. It's important to have a mental roadmap, but patience is also essential. See http://www. inc.com/howard-tullman/why-you-need-a-reverse-roadmap.html

He also noted that his father was a source of both instruction and inspiration. Bill said that one of his father's principal rules was that "practical execution" was what really mattered in the end. All the talk was simply that – results and actions were the things that made a difference. His Dad used to say: "show me, don't tell me" or as I like to say: "you can't win a race with your mouth". Less talking and more typing is how things get done. And it won't ever happen if you don't get started. There's no simple playbook or set of rules for how you invent the future – you've got to get the ball rolling, keep your eyes on the goal, and be agile and flexible all the time.

Bill said that when we're born – we're only afraid of two things – falling and loud noises. We're the ones who learn to be afraid of other things and who too often let those fears keep us from stepping out and taking the kinds of risks that are essential for entrepreneurs to succeed. He quoted Emerson as saying that you needed to do what you are afraid of and that – if you do – success will find you. And as far as risks, he said that the key was to recognize and manage reasonable risks so that you could convert them into opportunities and rewards – not to try to avoid every possible risk. The ship that stays in port is always the safest, but it rarely accomplishes anything.

And finally he talked about the business with the bumblebee. He said that for years scientists have been saying that bees were never supposed to be able to fly because the ratio of the size of their wings to their body weight was all wrong. According to the "laws" of physics that meant that they could never have enough power to lift themselves into the air. Bill's point was that – just like so many entrepreneurs who do every day what others thought was impossible – no one ever told the bees that they couldn't fly and, accordingly, off they went.

But there's an important sequel to the story. Today no one says any longer that the bees are defying the laws of physics or nature because we have finally figured out that – just because the bees don't fly in the same way that fixed-wing airplanes do – doesn't mean that rules of gravity have been suspended for them. The fact is that bees – just like entrepreneurs – have figured out (with a little help from Mother Nature) a different way to solve the problem. They fly by rapidly rotating their flexible wings and that's how they get themselves off the ground.

Every day entrepreneurs are doing the same thing – we look at the same problems that millions of others have observed from new and different perspectives – and come up with novel solutions which are often obvious in retrospect. This is because we don't ask why; we ask why?

And when you do you'll see that not every niche leads to nirvana.

THE NEXT BIG EMPLOYEE PERK

Sometimes you just smack yourself in the head and say to yourself "why didn't I think of that?" It's so obvious and so right. But, of course, that's what makes great entrepreneurs. Entrepreneurs don't know what's impossible or what they can't do. They don't color within the lines or stay stuck in their silos. They see what everyone else has seen (and lamented for years); they think about it differently; and they bring a new perspective/approach to the problem. And then – in retrospect – it's blindingly clear to all of us. As Nelson Mandela used to say: it always seems impossible until it's done.

For years, I've been depressed by the fact that millions of people are trapped in crappy, dead-end jobs (yearning to be free to try to do something meaningful and important) because they are imprisoned by their need to preserve their company-based health insurance coverage for themselves and their families. It's hard to imagine the economic impact and the creative forces that would be unleashed if the futures of so many weren't fettered by the bonds of the bozos who run the health insurance scams in this country. (See http://www. inc.com/howard-tullman/why-wiki-work-is-the-future.html) This is in part why 1871 became the first mega-incubator in the world to offer health insurance programs for its member companies although – truth be told – almost all of our entrepreneurs think they're immortal and indestructible as well so they're more concerned about innovation than insurance in their day-to-day lives.

Now I'm not naïve and I do realize that "portable" health insurance and increased employee mobility isn't exactly a high priority on the lists of any of the major corporations in this country who are plenty concerned as it is with (a) motivating and hanging on to their good young people and also with (b) trying to figure out how they can attract the next several generations of smart, skilled newbies to their big, old and somewhat tired businesses. I don't see their HR departments rushing any time soon to get rid of the insurance handcuffs.

But, there's actually good news out there for everyone and a new solution that will serve both the existing young employee workforce and also be a sure-fire attractor for new talent. Forget free Frosty Melts, gym dues and mid-day massages – the new great employee perk – for businesses big and small – is right before our eyes. And the best news is that it's something you can get started on tomorrow whether your revenues are billions or bupkes. So even the big guys can do some good for a change by doing good for their employees.

In my daily conversations with dozens of techies in their 20s and 30s, it turns out that the real problem for almost all of them is not insurance, it's their substantial student debt. Frankly, no one cares about their 401(k) when they're worried about foraging for food on a weekly basis. In fact, a staggering number of young workers these days don't make any 401(k) contributions even when their employers are willing to match them.

So a new company based at 1871 (Peanut Butter) has come up with a simple, straightforward way for businesses to help their employees (new and old) get this brutal burden off their backs. Keep in mind that 40 million Americans have student debt right now and it averages over $30,000 a person. So this isn't just a new employee recruitment tool; it's also a powerful and proven retention tool to help keep your proven people around the place years longer.

And believe me, in this competitive recruitment market (where only a few companies can afford ridiculous signing bonuses and other incentives), you don't want your company to be the last one on the block to be offering this important helping hand to your best employees and hottest prospects.

Talk about a magnet for Millennials – this is the real deal – and these kids in particular are saddled with more student debt than any generation that came before them. Over 70% of the Class of 2015 graduated with student debt.

By 2020, Millennials will represent almost 50% of the total U.S. workforce. Surveys already indicate that most of the major employment decisions that new graduates are making are informed by the impact of their choices on their student debt including industry selection, job acceptances, and relocation options. If, as an employer, your benefits offerings aren't in the competitive set; you can bet that you'll be on the outside looking in at the competition as the best candidates head elsewhere.

Peanut Butter (www.getpeanutbutter.com) is a benefits administration business that makes it easy for employers of any size to make contributions to help their employees pay off their student loans. It's all online and everything from establishing the plan, signing up qualified employees, confirming loan amounts and determining contribution amounts, and even routing, tracking and documenting the payments being made are all incorporated with detailed real-time reports. Treasury management services are provided by a large and long-established Chicago-based financial institution.

Needless to say, this is an almost impossible task for an individual company regardless of their resources to undertake (even with the best of intentions) because every single employee's story is different and there are literally tens of thousands of different lenders, payers, borrowers, etc. It's an ideal use case for a one-stop, cloud-based platform business where all the investigation, standardization, documentation, payment programs and infrastructure are already built and in place so that it becomes a turnkey solution for each of the businesses who want to provide the service to their employees.

You could always try to do this yourself, I guess, but it would be a stupid use of your energy, time and resources when the solution is already sitting there. And an even dumber thing to do would be to wait until everyone else is already offering the benefit to their people. Just remember the old adage – when it's obvious that you need to change; it's probably already too late to do so.

TAMING THE TOWER OF BABEL

I mentioned in a recent INC. blog piece about Peanut Butter, a student loan repayment service for employers (www.getpeanutbutter.com), that one of the most compelling reasons I expect their startup to be successful was that they were creating a solution that virtually all of their future customers would eventually desire, and, at the same time, solving a problem which none of those prospective customers would or, for the most part, could solve for themselves and their own employees.

Interestingly enough, this dilemma wasn't because the customers (large or small) lacked the technical abilities to take on the problem of documenting, servicing and helping to pay down millions of unique student loans for their employees all across the country. It was due to the fact that it wasn't remotely worth the time or effort for any one of them individually to devote the necessary personnel, funding and other resources in an attempt to solve the problem. And yet, it was a very desirable competitive offering with obvious pent-up demand, a low-cost (and possibly pre-tax) incentive that they would love to offer to their employees, and it was clearly an attractive recruiting and retention tool as well. (See http://www.inc.com/howard-tullman/making-student-debt-less-sticky.html)

The most striking fact was that it was the very uniqueness of each loan and each employee's situation which made it inefficient and uneconomical for any one business to take on the problem. But, at the same time, in the aggregate, this problem was a large source of growing concern for more than 40 million student and parent debtors (as well as their employers) and a wide-open and lucrative market for the entrepreneur(s) who could provide an effective remedy.

I like to say that a bunch of tiny little problems (seemingly nuisances not worth anyone's time or trouble) can very often roll up into quite a substantial opportunity. And, believe me, there's nary an industry out there where you won't find similar aggregation opportunities if you take the time to look.

We see this kind of widely-distributed, but unaddressable pain in all kinds of political and community situations where the powers that be just can't or won't be bothered to try to build a solution and no individuals have enough of a stake (or enough at stake) to take on the larger problem for the good of all. Everyone suffers, but no one typically cares enough to step up and try to solve the problem.

Of course, at least in the area of tortious business conduct, and but for the fact that most class action lawyers are scumbags, this was exactly why the vehicle of class litigation came into being so that a few representative and committed plaintiffs could act on behalf of the interests of an entire class of injured parties. Unfortunately, the overwhelming outcome in 99% of all class action cases is that it turns out that the only parties whose interests are being served are the lawyers. The bad guys may sometimes be modestly punished, but the good guys who are the actual victims generally get squat. But I digress.

The real moral of this story is that there are a couple of underlying principles at work here which have universal application and value and, if you can identify how they present themselves in an industry that's of interest to you, and you can quickly build a low-cost solution (at least at the outset) that can massively scale as demand grows, you can ultimately create a very large and profitable business. The principles and the patterns are there in every marketplace. At 1871, we have companies (in addition to Peanut Butter) dealing with similar issues in education (Learnmetrics), funds transfers (Pangea), social services (mRelief), etc.

More and more of these kinds of problem situations are being created every day as the flow and volume of mission-critical data accelerates and the complexity of all data-driven marketplaces grows exponentially. The confusion in formats, inconsistent language and terminologies, conflicting or competing vendors who refuse to adopt common conventions and methodologies, and similar problems which preclude straightforward and efficient communication and the rapid transmission of critical information have created Towers of Babel in dozens of industries. These present nothing but great opportunities for clever and ambitious entrepreneurs to build one-stop solutions. It's their job to find and address the pain points in new marketplaces and to do it before someone else does.

What are the basic market characteristics that you need to look for?

(1) There are no industry standards, common measurements, or terminology, but effective normalized communication between the parties is increasingly critical.

(2) There are no central hubs, channels or clearing houses to locate and access the vast amounts of data being generated and the data exists in multiple, inconsistent forms and formats.

(3) Individual industry members aren't incented or otherwise motivated to act on their own either independently or in concert and/or may be legally prohibited from doing so.

(4) The industry desperately needs consistent data and objective documentation to authentically and accurately measure and report its progress and performance to multiple regulatory and funding constituencies.

What are the components of the solution you need to build?

(1) You need to aggregate, translate and standardize the diverse data and different inputs so you can accommodate all the alternatives out there.

(2) You need to be the one-stop shop and the simple solution that all the players can share regardless of their levels of sophistication and technology.

(3) You need to invest in the infrastructure and build the broad and scalable backend that no one else has the bucks or the balls to build.

(4) You need to build it before any of the big guys finally figure it out so that you're the benchmark for the business and their best bet is to buy you.

This is one of those rare environments and moments in time where the Field of Dreams isn't a dream. If you build it right; if you're just a little patient; they will come.

4 LESSONS FROM THE FIRING LINE

W hew! We're thisclose to getting our new 1871 3.0 build-out project done where we're expanding our Chicago facility by more than 50% to create more space for startups, schools and sponsors. It's typically a mixed bag of relief and euphoria when you bring one of these big budget babies in on time and on the money. And right now, before the next wave of activity and the next crisis rolls around, I'm just happy to take a breath once in a while, push out my blog posts, and wait for the fresh paint to dry.

Growing your business is always a challenge regardless of what stage you're in and it can be a blessing and a curse all at the same time because one thing's for sure – more isn't always better by a long shot. And not all motion or commotion moves your enterprise forward. I believe that construction projects (they're virtually unavoidable at some point in your business) are among the most painful parts of the company growth process. They're all non-stop, on the fly, mission-critical streams of big and small decisions - all of which are time- and money-sensitive – and most of which are harrowing and tough cases of "either-or" choices where you're usually trying to build the Taj Mahal on a Taco Bell budget. It's the old sad story of "Pick Any Two": your project can be (1) done well, (2) done on time or (3) done on budget – totally up to you. Of course, if you're a good entrepreneur and you're like me, you simply say that you don't have to make these false choices and bad decisions – you would simply like to have it all. Not easy, but essential.

And – regardless of the pain in the middle of the project - when the drywall dust finally settles and the last of the painters packs it in, you'll discover that the whole adventure has taught you some very important and basic lessons that you will put to use in building your business for many years to come. Everyone learns (and earns/deserves) their lessons in their own way (and in their own time) and everyone's lessons are a little bit different based on their circumstances, but after building out more than a quarter of a million square feet of new space over the last few years with some very important help at my side, here are a few hard-earned notes that I'm happy to share with my fellow entrepreneurs.

1. Nobody cares as much as you do.

Entrepreneurs need to take this stuff - every last bit of it - personally and to heart. I always say that the one who cares the most wins. That will never change and the people who tell you "it's just business" are the ones who always end up eating dust and watching the doers fly by. Caring enough and being willing to show it - without apology or embarrassment - and insisting that there's always a right and best way to do even the hardest things without compromising is hard, every day work. It's easy to get down at times and worn out as you keep pushing those big ugly rocks up the hill, but it's the perspiration and the perseverance that separates the great ones from the also-rans and the people who are willing to settle for second best. If you continue to consistently insist on the best, you'll be amazed what you end up with. In the end, people commit to other people and sign up for their dreams – not only because they want to be a part of something great and bigger than themselves – but also because dedication, enthusiasm and caring are the most contagious things around. You'll also find that you can't do this all by yourself and so it's absolutely crucial to have people on your team and at your side whose "take no prisoners" attitudes are the same as yours. But they're not gonna be the most popular people in the place and so another part of your job is to run interference for them and have their backs when they go to bat for you and the project because a whole boatload of folks will have it in for them from the beginning. You want people who soar, not people who settle, at your side.

2. No one pays attention like you do

It turns out that - if you're out of sight, you're out of mind. Being there - in the moment and in the thick of things - is always better. Paying attention is an art and you can't phone this stuff in. As the Chinese say: All things flourish where you turn your eyes. It not only shows that you care a lot - it shows that you're also willing to roll up your sleeves and do whatever it takes to get the job done. Most architects don't get this concept and - as a result - instead of nipping things in the bud and in the moment because they're on the site and on the job - their attitude is that - if something is done wrong, we'll just waste precious time, a lot of energy, and someone else's money on finger-pointing, extensive CYA documentation, and then they order "do-overs" instead of concentrating on "do-rights" the first time around. It's a disgusting and wasteful approach and it makes the guys who matter - the client and the contractors - very unhappy. Enough "do-overs" can suck the contractor's profit and enthusiasm right out of the project and then you – the owner-client – are really screwed because no one wants to be working for nothing. If you want people to care and try to do their best, your best bet is always to be there right beside them and – at the same time - to do whatever you can to keep the "professionals" from messing up the program. Very often, in the end, that means that you have to do their job (or rather the job they should be doing) for them.

3. No one sweats the small stuff like you

If you always sweat the small stuff, the big things tend to take care of themselves because they're built on a solid foundation where the details make all the difference. Compromise is a crafty beast and shamelessly sneaks up on you whenever you take your eyes off the ball - even for an instant. It's a very slippery slope and it's easy to lose your way because the first cut turns out to be the easiest not the deepest and then it's all downhill from there. The people who complain about micro-managing have never built anything special in their shabby and second-rate careers and their shortcuts always show in the end. It turns out that it's easier to be 100% on the program than it is to settle even slightly for less than the best. And you will be totally amazed at how easy it is to make the right calls and decisions - however many there may be - when you stick to your guns and your values throughout the process.

4. No one is a bigger noodge than you

People certainly need instruction from time to time, but what they really need is to be reminded constantly of the central goals, the key directions and the main chance because - in today's short attention span world - even the people who are listening aren't necessarily hearing what you're saying or remembering what's most important when the chips are down and the going gets rough. It's your job to make sure the messages are getting through and that means being obsessive, being overly and redundantly communicative, being omnipresent, backstopping everything, and always being attentive. And, of course, doing it that way every day.

In service businesses today (and, by the way, every business is a service business today or it won't be a business for long), you don't get a chance to consult the manual or a second chance to make a first impression. Your people are on the firing line from the get-go and the idea of a rule book and standard operating procedures is a joke because nothing's standard any more. Trying to set up rules and responses for every case is a crazy waste of time and doesn't remotely relate to the pace and the extent of the disruption that every business is facing every day. The days when you could "set it and forget it" or let anything run unattended for any period of time are long gone. And your people have to react right now wherever they are and whenever the client or customer wants answers and doesn't want to wait. This isn't an easy environment for anyone and mistakes are bound to be made. No one hates mistakes more than I do, but what you learn over time is that it's more important to be a constant and constructive coach for your people than to constantly be a judge or an umpire.

STARTUP LESSONS FROM
SUPER BOWL 50

For me the Super Bowl had so many of the unfortunate characteristics and reminders of the kinds of struggles that every startup goes thru that - by the game's anti-climactic end - it felt surprisingly like just another day at the office. It was more like an obligation than an opportunity. You had to watch it, but no one really expected that you would enjoy it. And the commercials were not much better. The game was much more of a sideways shuffle than a spectacular show and there certainly wasn't a lot of "joy in Mudville" for anyone on either team. It wasn't a thrilling competition between two super-closely matched competitors – it was more like a contest to see who could make the fewest mistakes and still put some points on the board. There's no passion in playing to avoid the potholes rather than shooting for the stars.

Building a business can feel like a similar grind for days and months on end, but those are the times that it pays to keep your head down and keep plowing straight ahead since that's what will make all the difference in the long run. Playing it safe – trying to straddle the middle – going for maintenance rather than majesty – all leads you to the same sorry state. This startup stuff is hard – it's not for the faint-hearted - and not everyone gets a trophy for trying really hard or a salute for showing up. You've got to set the bar high – model the necessary behavior every day – and never let them see you sweat.

Anyone who tells you that being an entrepreneur is a lot of "fun" hasn't been there and is most likely lying to you. It can be thrilling and super satisfying; it can be exhilarating and enervating; it can also be downright lonely and depressing, but it's always work – not fun. Fun is what you theoretically do on your own time – as if there was such a thing in the startup world.

On Sunday the good news was that everyone survived - not too many injuries or concussions – but also not many points on the score board for long stretches - not a lot of glory plays or great stands or saves - and not exactly an inspiring contest likely to stir men's blood. It felt like the winners were more relieved to escape with their modest victory and some dignity than ecstatic about how they triumphed. And sometimes in the startup world, you can get to the end of a week where you wonder how you even made it through and ended up still standing only to discover that you didn't really accomplish a damn thing in terms of moving the business forward. The truth is that today it takes more than baby steps and incremental improvements to change the game and move the needle. The future isn't going to be incremental – it's going to be explosive. What we don't know is just whose efforts are going to be the ones that make the real differences – the hustlers, the hipsters or the hackers. But whatever the team consists of, it's headed nowhere without a leader that the rest of the folks can believe in.

I think in a way that some of the disappointed feeling that surrounded the conclusion of this grossly over-hyped "big game" is an unfortunate commentary on how hard it is in our stupid celebrity-soaked system to root for a great defense rather than celebrating an amazing offense. Just like in a startup, the sales guys get all the kudos for bringing home the bacon while the coders just catch a lot of crap when the system shuts down. No one said that life was fair, and the linemen always come last, but who honestly really remembers that the most important touchdown in Sunday's game was scored early on by the defense. If you're in it for the credit, you're in the wrong place. To win, on game day and in business, everyone has to show up and do the very best job that they can – regardless of their responsibility or position – and know that they helped make a difference. No one does anything major these days all by themselves.

I guess it just goes to show you that you and your own team had better learn to appreciate and take your everyday satisfaction from all the preparation, perspiration, passion and hard work that you put into what you're building together (which you desperately hope will be special) regardless of the near-term outcomes and results because the world in general doesn't really care and no one gives you any points in the end for trying. "Almost" counts in love and horseshoes, but not so much in the real world of business.

Worse yet, just as we saw in the game on too many occasions, what you've put together and pushed painfully forward in your business can also be pissed away in a matter of seconds. There were mistakes and mishaps galore, foolish errors and omissions, sacks and stupid choices, taunts and other bad behavior that killed critical drives, and wastes of hard-to-come-by momentum throughout the game - virtually everything we also see in the startup world every day.

Now I can pretty much forgive a fumble or a missed field goal because those almost never arise from a lack of trying. As often as not, the main cause of a fumble is because the runner was trying to press for a few more yards and gets stripped or hit so hard that he loses the ball. But a lack of commitment or a failure of leadership is something that no team or business can accept for long. It's corrosive and contagious. For me, the saddest thing about Sunday's Super Bowl wasn't Cam Newton dropping the ball; it was that he stood there (while America and the world watched with bated breath) and didn't throw himself into the fray. He was deciding, not diving. Looking, not lunging.

And we were all sitting at home on the edges of our seats screaming "go for it", "get the ball" and he didn't do a thing. In fact, I'd say that the key to the ultimate moral victory in the game (forget what the score ended up being) really came down to that single play - a few painful and probative seconds - which may not have changed the final outcome, but that forever changed my impression of Cam Newton. And I'm willing to bet it changed the impressions of millions of other viewers as well.

When the moment arose and he was tested, he didn't step up – he hesitated – or worse, he took a pass. Maybe it was heart that he didn't have. Maybe he was saving himself for next season. Maybe he just didn't want it as bad as we wanted him to. But, whatever the reasons or the excuses, it wasn't what we expect from our leaders, and it was a sobering lesson for any startup.

You can't lead from the back seat or the bleachers. You've got to be in the moment – all-in – showing your people and your team that you care more than other people think is smart or safe. That you demand of yourself and them more than others think is practical or possible. And that when the window is there and the opportunities arise; you'll be the first one through to take the chances and seize the moment.

5 TIPS FOR STARTUPS FROM THE CUBS TALENT STRATEGY

The Chicago Cubs are having a spectacular season (so far) and, without taking anything for granted, it's clear that their talent strategy and their commitment to rebuilding the whole team with young, healthy impact players have begun to pay serious dividends. For a team that feels like it's been around forever and waiting to win big for almost as long a time, the Cubs also look an awful lot like a scrappy startup and a work always in progress where everything is up for discussion (and change) if it's likely to move the mission forward.

We had a chance recently to hear a lot of "inside baseball" talk from a couple of the management players in the Cubs organization and there were a few key takeaways from their experience that I think will be just as valuable for whatever business you're building. Keep in mind that these are simply my observations about what's going on and what's behind the rebirth and their improving fortunes. There's nothing "official" about what follows, but it does come directly from a few of the horses' mouths.

Creating the right culture and reinforcing the commitment of everyone in the organization to winning the World Series were two of the higher level and very central themes of the conversation. This reminded me of the early days of 1871 in some important ways. When we began discussing and defining the culture of 1871 and the special community which we hoped it would become, we spent a substantial amount of time on issues of governance. As you would expect from a group that included a number of successful and outspoken entrepreneurs, there were plenty of competing ideas and lots of loud opinions. Entrepreneurs don't always color within the lines or act like grownups and – of course – that's part of their enduring charm. But – if you're not careful - it can also make for a messy environment which is disruptive in all the wrong ways.

I'd say that ultimately we ended up opting for a basically Miesian "less is more" approach with just a few red lines. If things worked out well, 1871 would be a place driven by the right attitudes rather than by rigorous authority. I like to think that my biggest contribution to the whole process was a single sentence. I said that "a great culture has to be built on expectations of performance, not rules of behavior". We couldn't have written a master rule book even if we wanted to for an enterprise which was very much a grand experiment that we fervently hoped would become a self-sustaining and organic ecosystem. The Cubs have some of the very same challenges - to pull the broadest possible community into the park - to change the surrounding neighborhood for the better - and to make the entire country sit up and take notice of what is happening in Chicago.

As I listened during our meetings to the details of the Cubs approach, I was struck by the similarities to our own 1871 philosophy – the Cubs way was all about building a winning team for sure – but the foundations and the manner in which the ultimate goals would be achieved were all about the individual's responsibility for (a) controlling their own behavior; (b) improving their own performance (there would be plenty of help, but they needed to provide the heart); and (c) contributing to the greater good which meant specifically the players putting the team's success ahead of their own.

I came away having identified 5 basic strategic steps that I think are working for the Cubs and which are a helpful framework for anyone building a new business as well. Keep in mind that these things don't propagate themselves and that consistently communicating them to the members of your team and the broader world of third party stakeholders is a crucial and ongoing part of the success of the system. Everyone wants to know where they're going and how they're gonna get there and also wants to be sure that they won't be going alone. Equally important today for the younger players and team members is overt recognition and reinforcement - delivered authentically all along the way. Silent gratitude doesn't mean squat. Money is always nice, but acknowledgement and appreciation are the real drivers for young people these days.

So here are the 5 "simple" steps.

(1) Set the Team (Talent)

The up-and-coming ballplayers are the building blocks of any business's future and you're got to get and/or grow the best possible raw material for your team as cost-effectively as possible which - in the major leagues - actually means as early as possible. It's too bad that there's not a farm club system for every industry and this is a real issue for startups because you have to manage a mix of energetic young people and experienced older folks when you're growing quickly since not everyone can be learning the ropes of your business as they go. OJT is great, but too many people with too much rope can hang your company out to dry.

One really important thing to note is that the Cubs aren't just looking to recruit and grow their own talent on the field – they're applying the same approach to every part of the organization. In a business like baseball that is so people-centric throughout the whole organization, the gap in impact and effectiveness between a good team member and a great team member isn't 2X; it's more likely 5X to 10X because, in a service business, everything happens every day on the front line and there's no time to consult a rule book or a manager – you've got to go with your gut (and with what you've been taught, seen and internalized) and you've got to use your best judgment in the moment since you won't get a second chance to make a first (very critical) impression.

Initiative, creativity and empathy are force multipliers and the hardest challenge in an expanding and rapidly-growing people business is to keep these qualities alive in your team members as they age, grow and progress in your organization.

(2) Set the Table (Tools)

If you don't give your team the best available resources, tools and technologies which they will need to be successful (within whatever your realistic cost constraints may be), you're asking them to work with one hand tied behind their backs. This won't get you very far. The Cubs are spending over $600 million just on bricks and mortar in order to leapfrog the entire league and move from a sorry last place to the number one position in the country (if not in the world) in terms of athletic facilities, training and rehab resources, technology, nutrition, etc. I've seen the new spaces and they are astonishing.

Here again, there's an underlying element that is critical. My good friend, Harper Reed, who is awesome always says that – contrary to popular opinion - building a great corporate culture isn't about snacks, hammocks or foosball – it's about creating an environment where talented people who respect each other can work together to take on important challenges and make a difference. Respect is the key word.

The Cubs set aside a substantial empty space in their new clubhouse digs for the players' lounge, but then the designers stepped back and let the players decide exactly what screens, games, instruments, etc. would be in their lounge and how it would be set up. This wasn't about toys or technology – it was about respect for the players' opinions, their downtime, and their desires and giving them some ownership in the overall process and the outcome. The players' pride in "their place" is palpable.

(3) Set the Schedule (Timing)

Nothing this big or this costly happens overnight, but something happens every day and everyone notices. In our world today, if you're not moving forward, you're losing ground to someone. Momentum means more than size or scale. An ounce of momentum is worth a pound of acceleration. So it's critically important to put some concrete stakes in the ground and then to hit those targets. They don't have to be moonshots – they can be small, solid steps, but they need to point people in the right direction and show them that the wind is at the business's back and that things will only get better from here. And these milestones need to be recorded and celebrated throughout the business on a regular basis. Lastly, it's death to overpromise and under deliver. If you want people to believe your promises about tomorrow; it helps to have kept your word from yesterday.

(4) Set and Manage the Metrics (Thermostat)

What gets measured is definitely what gets done. Even more importantly, there's no sway and no confusion when you're talking about performance against previously agreed-upon goals and standards. You make your numbers or you don't. And there's really no such thing as a good excuse in a well-run business. Or getting by by blaming the other guys or laying it off on circumstances beyond your control. You take your medicine and you move on, but you also take away and apply the lessons going forward.

If you're gonna sit by and watch things happen to your business, you might as well be sitting in the bleachers. It's not enough to be the thermometer and just passively record the results; the best managers are thermostats whose actions raise the heat and improve the outcomes.

This may seem a little easier to do in a game that tracks at-bats and hits and runs than in your industry, but every business needs to develop effective and relatively frictionless ways to keep score for everyone's benefit and also to establish and implement these criteria at every level and for everyone in the business. The continued emergence of new and inexpensive measurement technologies is making this responsibility easier and more essential all the time.

(5) Step Back (Trust)

Once you've put everything in place, there's another critical element in the process that really separates the winners from the copycats and the folks who are just going through the motions. You can't "ape" your way to a winning culture. You can't buy a mission statement that means anything real down at the mall. You need two-way trust. You have to take a step back and trust your players and your people to get out there and get the job done.

You can't do it for them. In fact, you can explain things to them – over and over again – but you also can't understand this stuff for them. You can talk your way into their heads, but it's what's in their hearts that makes all the difference. They have to know three things: that you trust them; that the system is objective, not subjective; and that you've got their backs – rain or shine – as long as they give it their all.

WHEN'S THE RIGHT TIME FOR THE CEO TO STOP SELLING?

I realize that, if we were only dealing with the conventional wisdom, the simplest and most straightforward answer to the textbook question of when a company's CEO should stop his or her day-to-day selling of the company's products and services would typically be "never".

It's not exactly the ABC rule ("Always Be Closing") from Glengarry Glen Ross (You can watch the classic Alec Baldwin speech here: https://www.youtube.com/watch?v=Q4PE2hSqVnk.) but it's pretty close. Maybe today we would call it the ABS rule. Always Be Selling. If you're not excited about your business and your prospects, why would you expect anyone else to be?

In a way, you can just think of it as the need for the management of any startup to be perpetually pitching and it always starts at the top. It doesn't matter who the target is (customers, prospects, investors, employees, etc.), there's always a story to be told and sold. Telling and selling. And the CEO (so the experts tell us) should always be out front succinctly selling the story, deliriously describing the dream, and rigorously rallying the troops. It's a basic part of the boss's job description and not one that anyone gets to delegate. No one knows your business better than you.

Now, as a general proposition, I would say that it's hard to disagree with this idea. If you're not out there and constantly on the case, you can be sure that a competitor will be happy to take your place. You can't sell anything sitting on your ass in your office and nothing today sells itself. And the truth is that the best CEOs are also great salesmen (or women) who could sell shoes to a snake, but that may not be their highest and best use for the business after a certain point in its development. That's really the key question – when does it make sense for the CEO to stop?

There's actually a pretty good answer to this question – one that's especially relevant for startups - and a pretty simple guideline which can help you determine exactly (a) when it's the best time for the business to start hiring some qualified sales managers and (b) whether the time is right for the CEO to take a step or two back from the front line, hand off the ball to the sales team, and bench himself so he can be doing better things for the business.

Timing is everything in building the right team for a new company and, notwithstanding the fact that most of the time people are too slow in bolstering their business with some seasoned seniors, it's just as bad to be too early as it is to be too late. Getting some "grown-ups" in place and up-to-speed before you really start to scale the business is a key success factor in your growth and the best possible insurance that you won't stumble along the way. You want people who could sell muzzles to dogs on your team, but not too soon. It's too costly to have them just sitting around while the product guys try to get things right and they hate it as well. The very best sales people take it personally and want to be out there selling every day.

So the proper timing to add some professionals to your team is not an easy or obvious decision. I like to say that, in cases like this, it seems that it's always too soon until it's too late. However, the good news is that I can definitely tell you (with some degree of confidence and certainty) when it's definitely too soon for a startup to add dedicated sales talent to the team.

There are two simple rules:

(1) You don't need a sales team until you're ready to scale; and

(2) You're not ready to scale until you've sold a LOT of the SAME stuff to a bunch of SATISFIED customers.

We all know that there's no real business without sales and satisfied customers, but not all sales are the same for all purposes. You've got to nail it before you scale it (confirm both product and market fit) and big businesses are never bespoke. That's why it's critical that the successful sales which stick be of the same basic product or service without costly customization, without one-off incentives or add-ons, without a whole lot of handholding, and without spending more to get them than you're ultimately putting in your pocket.

But what does this have to do with the CEO being out there selling? He or she needs to be out there selling until the concrete sets and the product or service is locked down and secure. Until you've had a dozen serious sales (with happy customers) and it looks like things are sticking and the dogs are eating the dogfood. If there are still open questions, if there are changes or mid-course corrections that must be made, if there are pricing concerns or additional critical features to be added; there's really only one person who can make those calls and it's critical that the inputs to the decision-maker be direct and ideally face-to-face from the market and the customers. No one will ever tell it to you straighter than a customer and you need to hear the unvarnished truth to ultimately get your offerings just right. But you can't fix things from afar – only from the field.

Salesmen who don't make sales are especially good at coming up with excuses and offering explanations and reasons why your stuff doesn't sell. The worst of them are the best at this because that's mainly what they do all day - they make excuses instead of sales. And in startups, especially in the early stages when everyone pitches in, a lot of people are trying to sell who aren't even "sales" people and who have little or no training. They try to "sell" because there's no one else around to do it. That's not a good place for any business to be. "Trying" doesn't drive "buying" in the real world – selling is a skill just like many others and not something you pick up in your spare time. See http://www.inc.com/howard-tullman/bring-back-the-peter-principle-please.html.

So it's easy for an entrepreneur to lose patience and rush to get some skilled help in this area. But it's smarter to make sure that you've got something real and solid for these folks to sell before you bring them in and turn them loose and ultimately that's a call that only the CEO can make.

WE DON'T KNOW WHAT WE KNOW

I can't tell you how many times I'm in a conversation or strategy presentation with the senior management team of a major corporation and one of the first topics which comes up is their frustration with the lack of effective internal communication and information sharing in their own company. I'm not talking about mushy mission statements or internal HR "touchy-feely" messaging; I'm talking about the hard core, operational data which you need to drive the business and – even more crucial – the kind of anecdotal material and other market inputs which often get talked about at the water cooler, but never make it upstream to the people who can react to the information and change things. Information has no value unless it's successfully communicated.

These execs literally say that they (as well as other critical in-house decision makers) don't know what their own organization knows and – try as they might – they haven't been able to devise an effective solution to make the current situation better. They acknowledge that - even in the best of businesses - the quality of information deteriorates as it rises in the organization. And again, this covers every kind of information that's important to the company – we're not just talking about critical research or new discoveries; it can be as mundane as meeting menus or engineers needing more microwaves in the café – it's anything that bears on and impacts the overall productivity and success of the business.

This system-wide breakdown results in: (a) missed opportunities, duplicative efforts and misdirected expenditures; (b) inappropriate communications, false starts and other initiatives which eventually need to be walked back from the brink; and (c) the old standby where "the left hand doesn't know what the right hand is doing". It's inefficient, it's unprofessional and beyond embarrassing, and frankly it's a growing competitive disadvantage for any business. Data is the oil of the digital age and, if you're behind the curve or only seeing part of the story, you're in serious trouble which is only likely to get worse. Data alone won't do it of course because more data isn't the same as better information. You need a system that turns data into information and information into knowledge. Knowledge only becomes power when it's used and – unlike every other part of the creation and production process in any business – growing knowledge isn't subject to the law of diminishing returns.

As the information flow in the outside world becomes more and more streamlined and comprehensive, not having timely and accurate data about your own internal operations, issues and activities is an enormous information gap which consistently results in wastes of time, resources and energy. It can demoralize your people; anger your customers; confuse your partners and vendors; and give aid and comfort to the competition. I tell our member companies at 1871 that only two words matter today – transparency and efficacy. A fair assumption is that everyone everywhere will know what you're doing and how well you're doing it and, if you don't, shame on you. You'd think that addressing this kind of shortcoming would be a priority, but the lack of existing tools or technologies to help address the problem has pretty much remitted it to being a known concern with no known solution. Apologies for the slightly Rumsfeld-esque reference.

There are several reasons for this persistent problem (which I would note is by no means restricted to "big" businesses) and this seems to be a recurring issue for millions of businesses regardless of how "open" a business claims to be. Some of the practical impediments to timely sharing are structural and logistical issues including cases where surveys may be manual, where the respondents are multi-lingual or where employees are widely distributed, in different time zones and/or in distant locations. Others are procedural or hierarchical where there may be a reluctance to confront more senior managers, sensitivities around relationships with other groups or departments, a culture that prefers peace to progress and quiet to confrontation, etc. And then there are the "kill the messenger" concerns where no one wants to be the one to deliver the bad news. Last, but not least, are managers who don't want to know. Even though confusion is a higher state of knowledge than ignorance, these are the folks who say: "don't confuse me with the facts". (See http://www.inc.com/howard-tullman/3-things-you-need-to-know-about-advertising.html.)

But there's good news on the horizon. An 1871 company, Baloonr (www.baloonr.com), has built a simple, self-serve, system that enables rapid-fire, company-wide, anonymous (but trackable) information, idea and feedback gathering from sources inside the company (as well as outside if desired) on a prioritized and confidential basis. Any group of any size can be accommodated at any time. Talk about a "right now" solution. It's already being used by a variety of large organizations - ranging from startups to universities to Fortune 50 companies - and the results have been impressive. My favorite quote from one of the early users was "it was like putting on glasses for the first time".

As proposals move through the system, advancing and being enhanced at the same time, they gain support and weight from various quarters and eventually they can be claimed and properly attributed to their authors. Credit ultimately goes to those to whom it is due and no one is penalized or stigmatized for suggesting ideas that didn't make the consensus cut.

As you might expect, the most immediate organizational advantage of the Baloonr system is actually the simplest. It's like a "secret ballot" on steroids. The initial cloak of anonymity makes it possible for everything to be shared without reservations (or personal consequences) and for the best suggestions and thoughts – regardless of origin or authorship – to be floated up to the top of the pile. (Pun intended.)

In addition, while we keep hearing about how the introverts are a great untapped resource at many companies, this system permits even the most reticent to participate and contribute for the greater good. All of the constraints relating to status, authority, gender, position, etc. are effectively removed and true collaboration is possible.

And finally, and even more importantly, high-speed iteration and building on the best ideas is enabled (again without positively or negatively "considering the source") with participants from across the entire enterprise joining and adding to the conversation.

If knowledge is power, Baloonr may hold the keys to the kingdom. Because today it's what you don't know that you don't know that can kill your business in no time at all.

"EXCEPTIONS" TO THE WRONG RULES

I never knock clichés. They wouldn't be repeated for decades by millions of people if there wasn't at least some grain of truth and inherent value in most of them. Even Yogi-isms (the "philosophical" observations of New York Yankee catcher Yogi Berra) always provided some genuine guidance. There's no stronger call to action than Yogi's famous advice: "when you come to a fork in the road, take it". Or, as we might say today: "don't just stand there, do something". And there's never been a clearer explanation of pattern recognition (which is so critical to making smart investment decisions) than when he opined: "it's like déjà vu all over again". And my favorite – as a former restaurant owner and operator – was his comment about the perils of excessive popularity. He noted that: "no one goes there nowadays, it's too crowded".

I was thinking about Yogi in a slightly different context recently when someone told me that a specific situation we encountered was the exception that proved the rule. The more I thought about it, and how he used the phrase, the more I wondered if he even understood what that expression actually meant. I'm not sure that most of us do.

It's like young lawyers who say "for all intensive purposes" when they mean "for all intents and purposes" or worse in cases where people butcher the lyrics of classic songs. Wrapped up like a douche (instead of deuce) was always my Springsteen example from Blinded by the Light. I realize that the lyric was actually written by Manfred Mann. But it will always be Bruce's song to me.

As it turns out that part of the reason for the confusion around the significance of exceptions to the rule is because we don't even reference the full phrase these days – we've dropped a critical part of the original language – because I think it seemed on its face to be so circular. The complete expression from ancient Rome actually states: "the exception confirms the rule in cases not excepted". This reminds me a lot of Humpty Dumpty saying to Alice about a word that: "it means just what I choose it to mean – neither more nor less." Whatever that means.

Still another part of the difficulty is that there are a number of different "accepted" understandings of the concept which vary (according to the scholars) in degrees of accuracy and correctness.

But what really interested me was a different concern which is important for every entrepreneur and that was the traps we can fall into when we make the bigger mistake of thinking that a single rule governs all of the cases in a given situation.

It turns out that there are rules that are common and applicable to regulating behaviors in industries that we think of as being quite diverse (like medicine and manufacturing) and then there are other different rules (rather than exceptions to the same general rule) that apply to govern other types of behaviors. It's not about good or bad apples – it's about being careful not to treat apples and oranges as if they were the same.

As you create your business's culture and identify and communicate the behaviors you want to encourage in your company, it's essential to start from a clear understanding of which rules make sense for the kind of business you're building and the industry you're in. And you need to understand as well that all the rules in the world won't ultimately get the job done unless you want robots inside of real people working for you.

The best businesses are organized around expectations of performance and not based on rules of behavior in large part because even the best managers can't be there all the time and you need your people to make the right calls in the moment – not run to or hide behind some massive rule book. Just like one size never fits all, your core beliefs have to closely and specifically align with what makes the most sense for you, your team, and your company. (See http://www.inc.com/howard-tullman/are-your-values-costing-you-too-much.html.) This is a process that's actually a lot easier than it sounds.

Let's take a simple example of what's pretty much understood as a "universal" rule/proposition which, I would argue, has next to nothing to do with the way that millions of entrepreneurs should run their businesses. The simplest way to state the basic concept is this:

Preventing Errors is Cheaper than Fixing Them

Hard to argue with this pretty conventional piece of wisdom. It's always cheaper to do everything right the first time. Not possible, but theoretically cheaper.

Of course, almost every car manufacturer would disagree with you. At least until they get caught lying about what they knew and when. Like poorly positioned exploding gas tanks or shrapnel-spewing airbags. Then they have no choice, but to fix the errors regardless of the cost. And, at that point, they rationalize it as a PR and marketing cost and not the result of a design or process problem or – worse yet – the end product of some stupid cost-cutting move that put profits above people.

But leaving the car guys aside, here's the crux of the question: in some businesses the smartest and most conservative course is error avoidance and, in others, it's the worst way you can proceed. Your job is to determine which is the right course for your company and – just to make things rougher – it may be that different strategies are right for different parts of the same business. Simple shorthand – we want new and faster bullet trains being built (innovation), but we want today's trains to run safely and on time (operation).

So how do you determine what's best for your business? Here are a couple of simple questions to ask yourself:

(1) <u>What is the fundamental deliverable of my business?</u>

    (a) <u>Goal A</u>: Is it providing a consistent and dependable outcome? Each and every time and as regular as rain. This would describe industries like manufacturing and professions like medicine? No one wants a cowboy for their cardiologist. Let them experiment and learn on someone else.

    (b) <u>Goal B</u>: Or is it providing new, unexpected and innovative results? Are my clients and customers looking for completely different ideas and game-changing creativity? This would describe industries like advertising (at least in the old days) and high-end fashion. Everything about successful fashion these days needs to be inspirational and definitely not institutional. Frankly, no one could wear the latest Parisian fashions even if they tried because – for the runway shows – they're mostly stuck together with tape and safety pins.

        Once you have figured out whether you're basically building an A or a B business (and yes I know that every business will have elements of both), then you need to ask yourself:

(2) <u>Am I building a system with controls and a bunch of procedures and processes to help my people deliver a fixed and expected result?</u> These are primarily businesses dominated by operational and managerial concerns. Error-free execution is essential. Process changes, innovations, and system improvements are normally outside of the day-to-day scope of operations. You will also need people to help you get better, but every day you need to take care of business.

(3) <u>Am I creating an environment that encourages experimentation, risk-taking and new approaches with all the errors inherent in that process that you would expect?</u> These are primarily businesses dominated by creative and developmental concerns. Leaps, not layups, are what it takes to succeed. Trying to avoid mistakes, avoiding embarrassment, and playing it safe is a formula for failure.

Once you know where you're headed and what you are building, you can decide how to focus your time and attention most effectively. It helps a whole lot to have a roadmap – especially if you care a lot about where you end up.

There's more to this discussion. But the critical thing is that the demands, the designs and the drivers of these two very distinct types of businesses are very different, and it's easy to confuse your objectives and commingle your approaches if you're not totally clear. No one business or single approach can be all things to all people.

If you're running a "factory"; rules, regulations and restrictions are your best friends.

If you're running an operating room; protocols, checklists and sterilizers will save lives.

If you want new ideas and novel solutions; you need stronger people, not more structure.

If you're building the future; you can't steal second base with one foot on first.

DON'T FINISH WHAT YOU START

I was recently asked what productivity tools, handy tips or other strategies I have used over the years to help me stay on course – focused on my most important goals and primary objectives - in the midst of the messy multitude of ongoing emergencies, unavoidable distractions and regular interruptions that make up my typical day. I wish I had a good answer or a magic wand to solve the problem, but I've yet to find a single approach or solution that works even most of the time. It's a constant battle and it only gets harder as your business and your responsibilities and the demands on your time grow.

I do think that it helps to ask yourself many times a day a simple question: is what I'm doing or about to do moving my business forward? If not, do something else. And I also think that it can be destructive and a very bad idea to ask yourself a different question - whether what you're being asked to do in the moment is the highest and best use of your time. That question is an ego trap and it becomes way too easy to quickly convince yourself that you're too good or too busy or too important to do some of the very mundane things that need to be done.

It may not be your specific job and it may not be the best use of your time in some purely economic sense, but some things just need to get done and it's important that people feel that you're more than happy and prepared to pitch in. This is not solely because critical work can't be left undone; it's also because the even bigger risk to your business is that the message which this kind of bad and arrogant behavior often sends is a culture killer. I pick up the trash all day long. I run the lion's share of my own errands. I answer my own phone. If I'm too good to do these kinds of things, why should anyone else care about getting them done?

Now I do think it would be nice to be King and simply get to set my inviolable schedule and stick to it like clockwork, but my business life is really no different than anyone else's and that's just not the way an entrepreneur's world ever works.

The best entrepreneurs try to steer a steady course forward through constantly changing and challenging circumstances. They fiercely protective of their time and they try to keep anyone else from controlling their calendar or their inbox. (See http://www.inc.com/howard-tullman/slow-down-it-might-save-your-business.html.) And they do have one more trick in their bag that makes all the difference. They know that they don't have to finish what they start. And you don't either – at least for right now.

But that's rank heresy you say. Even the Bible insists that we finish what we started (2 Corinthians 8:11) and I'm sure Shakespeare and Ben Franklin had a thought or two on the subject as well. Bear with me for a moment and think about the most productive people you know. They're absolute masters of constant triage – re-prioritizing things all the time and on the fly - and that's what keeps them rolling in the right direction.

They don't worry so much about square corners, neat piles and getting everything done exactly on time and to a T – they're focused on paying attention to what's most important for the business in the moment and that always taking precedence even if other tasks get left undone. Punctuality is much less important most of the time than productivity. It's a given that there's never enough time to get everything done and done well – part of the trick is that understand that not everything worth doing needs to be done to perfection. Good enough is often good enough and sometimes – left to their own – things will even take care of themselves.

Now I'm sure that it's more than a little frustrating to all those folks waiting in the wings or right outside the office – hoping that their request or project is still on the top of the pile – or worse yet – getting ready to dump some new problem in their boss's lap, but they're not the ones driving the train or setting the schedule and the best bosses make that distinction abundantly clear – early and often. It's OK to ask and it's even OK to push once in a while, but nagging is a no-no. For the moment, it is what it is. Down the line, we'll make it into whatever it will be. It's all about doing the right things and not worrying about doing things right.

So if you find yourself in a fix from time to time and feel a little like you're drowning in too many tasks, give yourself permission to give yourself a break and put the things that can wait to the side (even if they're not finished) so you can focus your energies and attention on the things that matter most at the moment.

LEADERS LEARN BEST BY LISTENING

These days we're constantly rushing from one thing to the next. All of us – all of the time. The days are ever longer and the nights are even worse. I call it a life of "playing the entire game in overtime". You might be kidding yourself and calling it masterful multi-tasking, but I'd say it's mostly just a mess. We're constantly trying to make time for everything and we're discovering that, not only is this an impossible dream, but – what's worse - is that we're ending up spending too much of our time on the urgent - rather than the important - things in our lives and in our businesses. More every day, we're losing sight of what really matters. Our inboxes (calls, emails and especially texts) are driving us instead of the other way around. The fact is that you'll never get into the flow if you're fighting non-stop fires all day long.

It's also abundantly clear that, as the speed of our days increases, we're losing the one-on-one people time necessary to connect with the others in our lives and in our companies whose thoughtful input we need to make smart decisions as well as the right choices for the future. I'm talking both about accessing crucial company data as well as not cutting off the far more critical access to the personal and emotional feedback we all need from those we work with in order to succeed. Sadly, with the rate of change in our lives accelerating every day, I don't see things getting better for us any time soon unless we start to take back some control, have a little patience, and slow the entire process down.

It starts with making time to listen. People will tell you the truth – which only hurts when it ought to – but only if you make it clear that you're interested and paying attention when they try to talk. Entrepreneurs all pride themselves on being great talkers with the "gift of gab", but it's much harder to sit still and listen. Even better, no one's ears ever got them into hot water.

Taking on and trying to do too many things at once makes for an unendingly stressful life and – even worse - mediocre results across the board for your business. It never pays to be a mile wide and an inch deep in anything. It might be worth the pain and the sacrifices if the bottom line results were there, but the evidence is all in the other direction. Trying to be all things to all people or please all of the people even part of the time is as impossible as trying to be in two places at one time. No one expects this of you (except maybe you) and – if you give them a chance – they'll tell you that and they can even help you get over some of the hardest spots. It's never smart to try to do everything. It's not remotely practical to try to do it all by yourself. And, in the end, it's a losing proposition for everyone because you inevitably find yourself trying to do a bunch of things poorly or cheaply that you shouldn't be doing at all.

"Hurry sickness" is definitely an occupational disease of entrepreneurs, but it's not incurable. Slow down, catch your breath, ask for some advice and help, and let your people do the talking. Wisdom and smart decisions are the rewards you get for listening when you would have much preferred to be talking.

There are two main reasons (apart from a continual lack of enough time and a constant lack of enough money) for the persistence of this particular problem and both can be addressed – maybe not entirely eliminated – if we just keep a couple of simple ideas in mind.

The first reason for the constant frenzy is because no one wants to slow down and be run over by their competitors and/or be left behind by their customers. Fast followers are lurking behind every bush just waiting to go to school on your example, create a faster, easier or cheaper solution, and quickly try to take your place. Customers' expectations are perpetually progressive – the bar never stops rising - and their demands will only continue to increase and ratchet up over time. You've got to be rapid and responsive, but not rabid.

It still pays to be paranoid and to try to keep constantly moving your products and services ahead (while iterating all the while), but speed alone isn't all that helpful if you're headed in the wrong direction. Not all movement (however frantic) is progress or even forward motion and too much trying can sap precious energy, waste critical and scarce resources, and take your eyes off the main chance. There's a right way to handle and prioritize these things, but a successful approach rarely starts with acting in the moment or reacting to the surrounding circumstances. It starts with listening and taking stock.

Looking for effective solutions without taking the time to carefully listen to your customers' problems is like working in the dark without a flashlight. A lot of coding and other activity may make your engineers feel better (it's a somewhat effective antidote for anxiety), but it's not likely to be moving the ball up the field or leading your business to a better result for your clients unless it's informed by actual and timely customer input. Making the time and taking the time to listen closely is not only smart business; it's the safest way to proceed because no one ever listened themselves out of a job.

The second reason that drives a lot of entrepreneurial excess has more to do with managing people's imagined perceptions rather than reality except that - in the intense context of a startup – perceptions and impressions are often long lasting and can quickly harden into unpleasant realities.

I'm a major advocate of leading by example and modeling the behavior that you expect from your team, but many entrepreneurs take this idea too literally and push it too far. They believe that, if you're too calm, too collected, or too unconcerned with today's crisis, your team members will think that you don't care or that you're not all-in. Ya gotta let them see you sweat so they'll know you've got some skin in the game right alongside theirs. And, to prove the point, they think they need to run around like crazy people all day long. They worry that, if they slow down or sit down, people will be suspicious of their commitment.

But the truth is that these are the very people trying to get your attention and also to get a word in edgewise. They'd line the floors with flypaper if they thought that would slow you down for a few seconds. They want to be heard and they want to be helpful and it's all up to you. Listening is the highest form of courtesy.

So give yourself a break, take some more time to listen, and – when you're drowning in a hundred contradictory suggestions and ideas - remember the cardinal rule: most of the time, it's far more important to listen to people's advice than it is to heed it.

MAYBE YOU'RE NOT THE BEST BOSS
FOR YOUR BUSINESS

I get that everyone wants to be the boss. But the truth is that very few people have the necessary set of emotional, technical and intellectual talents, skills and tools that it takes to succeed over time in building a new business. This is even more of an issue when you're trying to finance and grow a startup in the critical period when it begins to gain some traction and starts to scale. Sure, you can try to hurry out there and hire some grown-ups to help, but if you've got the wrong person in the driver's seat, you're never going to get the business to the next level. And sometimes, you're the only one who honestly knows that you're the wrong guy or girl for the job.

The list of what it takes to succeed is a long one and I've written about these various attributes before and how challenging it is to have to balance so many competing considerations at the same time. You've got to walk that thin line between pushing the envelope and being somewhat patient so that you don't get too far out over your skis and crash. You've got to be demanding and also delicate – getting the most out of your people isn't the same as getting the best from them. Making room for people is all about different strokes for many different folks. You've got to have a thick skin to ward off all the naysayers and know-it-alls so you can keep going and an open mind so that you can not only hear, but also listen to and learn from, well-meaning and smart people when they tell you what you're doing

165

wrong and how things will need to change in order for the business to grow.

And all the while, you've got to keep your head up high and not let anyone see you sweat or worry. Leadership is an ongoing performance art and you're never offstage. It's an all-consuming constant juggling act and it never slows down or gets easier. And because there are always so many different things going on, it's very easy to get spread a mile wide and an inch deep – to keep jumping from one crisis to another without taking a breath - and it's very hard to find the time to do what it is that you do best which isn't everything for anyone. But no one's gonna go out of their way to tell you that or to tell you to take it easy. It's all pedal to the metal and balls to the wall. They've all got their own agendas and going slow isn't anyone's idea of how to get ahead today.

And that's the really bad news – spending the lion's share of your time trying to be all things to all people, running around like crazy, and trying to do a little bit of everything that needs to get done may not be your highest and best use or the way that you can make the greatest contribution to the ultimate success of the business. But it isn't ever easy to admit to yourself or anyone else that you may not be up to the job you're in. And it's even harder to share the truth with the other people who also need to hear it. It's never easy to say what nobody wants to hear. And it's especially difficult and more than a little scary for any entrepreneur to acknowledge that maybe they're not the best person for the top job.

The Peter Principle is still alive and well – it's just slightly different and more complicated when the person who's the problem is also the founder or co-founder of the business rather than someone pushed or promoted into a position that's over his or her head. I'd call this problem the Founder's Fallacy. The idea that every talented engineer or coder comes equipped with the skills it takes (or even the deep-down interest or desire) to lead the business or that he or she will automatically grow those abilities as time passes is a foolish fantasy.

And oftentimes it's actually the entrepreneur who figures these things out first. But knowing what should be done, admitting it to yourself and getting it done are very different things. But, when corrective action is required, if you don't initiate the process and try to guide it; you can expect one of two outcomes: (a) the business will start to go sideways, stall out, and eventually fail; or (b) the investors will finally work up their courage (and overcome their own fears and reluctance) and they will come for your head. It's much, much better to get ahead of the wave than to get pulled under and washed out.

There isn't one approach or formula that fits every case, but there are three basic ground rules that govern this process and you need to work through them and see where you and your business stand.

(1) Be Honest with Yourself

We each have our own strengths and weaknesses. We need to play to them and not ignore them. But, even more importantly, each of us has things that we love to do and other things that we abhor and do poorly. The trick is to find the highest position possible where you still love doing what you're getting paid to do. Nothing is all fun and games (that's why they call it "work"), but the more time you can spend doing what you want to do, enjoy doing, and are really good at doing; the better the results for the business.

You need to ask yourself honestly if you're really enjoying coming to work every day or if you're increasingly frustrated because a million inconsequential things keep getting in the way of you getting the things done that you – and probably you alone – need to get done. If you're honest about it, you'll start thinking about getting someone else in there pronto so you can get back to taking care of the real business.

I'm watching this scenario play out in at least three young businesses right now. And every case is remarkably similar – you've got a guy who's great at analysis and data acquisition trying to deal with the banks and accounts payable – you've got a fabulous salesman trying to supervise day-to-day operations while he's standing on one foot at the airport waiting for his next flight to see a big new prospect – and you've got a guy who loves machines and hates people worrying about HR matters. It turns out – he's slowly learning - that even the smartest machines demand a lot less of you than people do. It's not a good thing that he hates people, but – for sure – dealing with people is not something he's good at.

The bottom line is that they need to quickly get real and make a better plan and they need to do it before their businesses fall apart or they get tossed out.

(2) Be Honest with Your Backers

Your Board and your investors won't pretend to be even slightly happy to hear that you want to hire your own replacement even though they may well be secretly relieved that they didn't have to force the issue. After all, this is really one of the only two things – overall strategy being the other - that they should be concerned with even though they generally spend way too much time in your shorts and in the weeds of the business.

But even if they're expecting it (or fervently hoping for it), this is still a complicated conversation that you need to handle exactly right. Any leadership transition is challenging even when the ship is steady and it's even more risky and perilous when the company is in the midst of a growth spurt. So expect everyone to be somewhat on edge including, of course, you.

To start out on the right foot, you're gonna have to get over your own feelings of failure and inadequacy which can quickly poison the discussion if you're not careful. You brought the idea to life; you got the ball rolling and now it's time to hand the reins over to someone else so that you can return to doing what you do best.

Be careful here that you don't get angry at the investors (or the world in general) for not appreciating you enough, not giving you the unlimited time and funds you needed to realize your dream, and/or not having your back and being disloyal to you (after all the sacrifices you've made for them) when the chips were down. I'm sure these sentiments are already familiar to you and that I'm not telling you anything new. But you have to put this stuff behind you. You need these guys on your side as much going forward as you did getting to this point.

You also have to deal with two additional emotional concerns and you need to convince the Board and the investors that you can successfully handle these feelings as well.

The first is the loss of control. Entrepreneurs are all about authority and control. So it's understandably very hard to let your baby go — even a little bit — and everyone who's been through the process knows how quickly problems can arise if there's not a clean and complete handoff. You can't have two CEOs and you can't set up a situation where your key people — for whatever reasons — start to shop for the answers/decisions that they're looking for from whichever one of you seems the likeliest to agree.

The second is the fear of being forgotten. Entrepreneurs very quickly get used to the spotlight, the strokes and the applause and it's hard to walk away. They don't want to be forgotten or no longer regarded as essential to the company's success. Sometimes this can turn into a serious problem where the prior boss acts in ways that sabotage the business. You would think that everyone involved was working in the same direction for the company's success, but human beings are a little more complicated than that. It's just a little satisfying to know that the guy stepping in to fill your big shoes isn't finding things quite as easy to pull off or as straightforward as they looked when you were running the show. The Germans may have invented the idea of schadenfreude, but it's alive and well in every C suite in this country as well.

The bottom line here is that you have to be out front and very clear with the Board and the investors that you're 100% on board with the transition plan and willing to do whatever it takes to make it work. One of the leader's most important jobs is to create the next generation of leaders.

(3) Be Honest with Your Buddies

The people who are going to be the most concerned and anxious about your decision are going to be the ones you are closest to and most dependent on. They're gonna feel abandoned, disappointed and more than a little angry that you're leaving them in the lurch - even if you're not. Sometimes the hardest part of being the boss and making the tough calls isn't fighting off your competitors; it's having to deal with the hurt feelings of your friends. But those feelings can't keep you from doing the right things for the business.

Startups are a lot like circuses and political campaigns. Intensely high-energy and high stakes exercises carried on in incredibly compressed timeframes. While the circus is set up and all over town; it's all bright lights, excitement and superstars. Once they strike the tents and move on down the road; it's an empty arena, some broken dreams and sawdust all around. Once a startup reaches a certain size and level of maturity, some of the early dreams and hopes (or delusions) also die and some of the people who got you there can't take you any further.

Political campaigns are even worse. You drive yourself and your team crazy trying to beat the other guys and then – when you win – the difficulties really begin because now you've got to make a series of impossible people choices and position selections and everyone in the running is someone who's been there from the start and helped you make it all happen. There are no simple answers and all the decisions are hard. But it's just another part of a job that no one ever said was gonna be easy.

The bottom line here – amid all the tears and hard feelings that will most assuredly be part of the process - is to be honest and to set out the circumstances and your choices as simply as possible. And then to remember that you can explain things to people, but you can't understand those things for them.

ABOUT THE AUTHOR

Howard Tullman is the CEO of 1871 in Chicago where digital startups get their start. He is also the General Managing Partner of two venture funds: Chicago High-Tech Investment Partners and G2T3V, LLC, which both focus on funding disruptive innovators. He is the former Chairman and CEO of Tribeca Flashpoint Media Arts Academy in Chicago. He is an active member of numerous city, state and civic boards and organizations and a tireless supporter and mentor to many start-ups and other businesses and individuals. He has successfully founded more than a dozen high-tech businesses in his 50 year career and created more than $1 billion in investor value as well as thousands of new jobs. He writes a regular weekly blog on The Perspiration Principles for Inc. Magazine and can be directly contacted:

- by email at h@1871.com
- on twitter @tullman
- his blog: tullman.blogspot.com
- his primary website: www.tullman.com

To get all of Howard's blog posts in one download, visit Blogintobook.com/tullman/.